Who We Are Now

Who We Are Now
Journeys across the United States
September 12, 2020–September 30, 2021

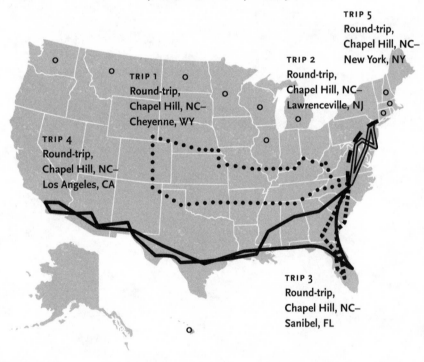

TRIP 5
Round-trip,
Chapel Hill, NC–
New York, NY

TRIP 2
Round-trip,
Chapel Hill, NC–
Lawrenceville, NJ

TRIP 1
Round-trip,
Chapel Hill, NC–
Cheyenne, WY

TRIP 4
Round-trip,
Chapel Hill, NC–
Los Angeles, CA

TRIP 3
Round-trip,
Chapel Hill, NC–
Sanibel, FL

o *Interviews conducted remotely via Zoom*

Who We Are Now

Stories of What
Americans Lost and
Found during the
COVID-19 Pandemic

Michelle Fishburne

....

Published by the University of North Carolina Press, Chapel Hill, in
association with the Center for Documentary Studies at Duke University

Set in Scala and Alegreya Sans
by Jamison Cockerham

Manufactured in the United States of America

Cover photo © iStockphoto/adamkaz.

LIBRARY OF CONGRESS CATALOGING-IN-PUBLICATION DATA
Names: Fishburne, Michelle, author. | Duke University. Center for Documentary Studies.
Title: Who we are now : stories of what Americans lost and found
    during the COVID-19 pandemic / Michelle Fishburne.
Other titles: Documentary arts and culture.
Description: Chapel Hill : The University of North Carolina Press ;
    [Durham, N.C.] : in association with the Center for Documentary Studies
    at Duke University, 2023. | Series: Documentary arts and culture
Identifiers: LCCN 2022029652 | ISBN 9781469671239 (cloth ; alk. paper)
    | ISBN 9781469671246 (ebook)
Subjects: LCSH: COVID-19 Pandemic, 2020—Social aspects—United States. | COVID-
    19 Pandemic, 2020—Economic aspects—United States. | LCGFT: Oral histories.
Classification: LCC RA644.C67 F56 2023 | DDC 362.1962/414—dc23/eng/20220715
LC record available at https://lccn.loc.gov/2022029652

DOCUMENTARY ARTS AND CULTURE

Edited by Alexa Dilworth of the Center for Documentary Studies at Duke University

In a time when the tools of the documentary arts have become widely accessible,
this series of books, published in association with the Center for Documentary
Studies at Duke University, explores and develops the practice of documentary
expression. Drawing on the perspectives of artists and writers, this series offers
new and important ways to think about learning and doing documentary work
while also examining the traditions and practice of documentary art through time.

Center for Documentary Studies at Duke University

https://documentarystudies.duke.edu/

A complete list of books published in Documentary Arts and Culture is
available at https://uncpress.org/series/documentary-arts-culture.

Dedicated TO THE PEOPLE I MET ALONG THE WAY

Contents

How This Book Came to Be

Meeting people during a pandemic is not easy. The sidewalks were "rolled up," as they say, in most of the towns I visited—even in big cities. When I drove my motor home into downtown Cincinnati at rush hour, there were hardly any cars at all on the bridge from Kentucky to Ohio. In fact, I stood in the middle of the road on that bridge for at least five minutes trying to take a good selfie. Only a handful of cars interrupted my efforts. Driving all over the country when hardly anybody is on the roads is surreal.

I set off on my *Who We Are Now* trek in September 2020. How I ended up doing this project is a story unto itself. In August 2020, I found myself without a house, a spouse, a job, or a kid to take care of, as my youngest had just left for college. I was fifty-seven years old and everything was upside-down. I moved into my 2006 motor home with the family dog, Buddy, and wondered what to do next.

One day while sitting in a Target parking lot, it occurred to me that I could do something like Brandon Stanton's *Humans of New York* project, only it would be about humans of the pandemic. The idea was to drive my motor home across the country and interview people about their lives and experiences during COVID—all the unexpected ways that they had been affected by it. My goal with *Who We Are Now* was to find out how people were doing, share their stories through social media, and hopefully become gainfully employed by January.

Rush hour in September 2020 on the John A. Roebling Bridge between Cincinnati, Ohio, and Covington, Kentucky.

....

When John Steinbeck set out with his camper and his dog, Charley, to cross the country in 1960, he wanted to answer the question "What are Americans like today?" What I wanted to know was who Americans were in the grips of a pandemic that locked us down, stopping life as we had known it. I was looking for a mosaic, not a conclusion. I wanted to see each of the pieces in the kaleidoscope through the individual voices of people from different walks of life, all over the country. If I could have talked to every single person in America, I would have, but I had to settle for traveling 12,000 miles and doing sit-down interviews with about 300 people. My question was simple:

What was your 2020 supposed to be like and what did it end up being like, through to the present?

That's the question I asked all 100 people you will hear from in this book. For most of the interviews, it was the only question. When I asked it, people would get kind of a faraway look in their eyes and they would talk for twenty-five, thirty, forty-five minutes. Then they would breathe. Politics was rarely mentioned. People

Buddy inside our 2006 Fleetwood Jamboree
motor home, which we fondly call "The Turtle."

focused instead on what mattered most to them—family, career, friends, community.

The majority of the interviews were done face to face, while others were done over Zoom or the phone. Transcription apps on my iPhone captured the audio of each interview. I used the transcripts to find key parts of each person's story to share on *Who We Are Now*'s website and social media channels. I added words here and there to smooth out the story and emailed the finished version to the person interviewed. Photos of the person were posted along with the story.

Finding people to interview was difficult in the beginning; the days of packed bars and bustling town festivals were a thing of the past. Before I arrived in a town, I would email organizations such as museums, nonprofits, and newspapers in hopes of talking with their employees. But you can imagine what it was like to get an email from a stranger who is traveling through your town during a pandemic and wants to interview you. Talk about intrusive. Hardly anybody answered my emails—not a big shock.

I started using Facebook to reach out to local businesses and organizations that had posted about recent events. I figured if they were sharing what they were doing online, maybe they would be open to talking with someone who had noticed their posts and wanted to talk about them. My first success was in Pine Bluffs, Wyoming. The parks and recreation director, who was in charge of the local kite festival, was nonplussed about why I would travel to Pine Bluffs just to hear about the festival, but when I explained what I was doing, she understood and began connecting me with other people in town. Connectors like her were really important to the project—they made their communities come alive for me, person by person.

When I finally figured out this Facebook-plus-local-connector approach, I started to have a good time. I left my heart in many places around the country, including Pine Bluffs, Wyoming; Raton, New Mexico; Shamrock, Texas; Henrietta, Oklahoma; Forrest City, Arkansas; Corinth, Mississippi; Scottsboro, Alabama; and Valdosta, Georgia.

It wasn't until late October 2020 that someone asked me, "Is this going to be a book?" "No" was my answer. I had never intended to be an author. Then a few more people asked me the same thing, and one person said, "Don't you realize that these interviews have historical value, that they are oral histories of people's lives during one of the world's most challenging times?" So in December I reached out to my alma mater's publishing house, the University of North Carolina Press, to see if they might be interested. You can guess the rest—my editor, Lucas Church, said, "Yes, it's a book."

I continued my travels into the spring of 2021, going from coast to coast and back, interviewing people along the way. I resorted to Facebook again to reach out to people I did not know. I also reached out to friends through Facebook and asked them to connect me with people in different states and with different backgrounds. A handful of additional interviews were done in the summer of 2021 in order to add particular types of stories to the mosaic of experiences. In September, I traveled to New York City for Broadway's reopening and did a few more interviews there. It seemed like a fitting way to end the book—in New York City, where, as the nation watched, the streets emptied and the hospitals overflowed in the pandemic's earliest days.

It was hard, frankly, to figure out which stories to include in this book. Fortunately, I had a trusted group of readers—friends, family,

Standing on "The Edge" in New York City in September 2021.

and the folks at UNC Press and the Center for Documentary Studies—
who helped me along the way. Each story is presented with just the
person's first name, state, and a brief description of their job (e.g., "hair
salon owner") or pandemic experience (e.g., "New York City resident
with COVID"). I chose to include minimal personal information and
no photos so that readers can focus instead on the person's words and
what they experienced. The stories are presented in a roughly chrono-
logical order based on when their particular experience happened as
the pandemic unfolded.

I am grateful to the people interviewed for this project; their

Enjoying the sunset from White Sands National Park (New Mexico) in February 2021.

....

willingness to let us see into their lives helps us to process what we ourselves went through during the pandemic. It is my hope that this collection of stories, this mosaic of experiences I found along my journey, will help us better understand the very odd road we traveled down together. Many people's lives were upended in surprising and sometimes devastating ways, while others' lives continued pretty much normally. Some people even found new life paths and new ways to think about how they want to live.

It has become a trite phrase at this point, but it is very true that "we are all in this together." Typing that phrase just now, I teared up remembering how often I heard it during my travels. People would say it and nod, in part to encourage others and in part to encourage themselves. The community of Forrest City, Arkansas, even had it on signs posted along its roadways. I wish you each could have been on my journey with me, there in the motor home, because I was truly fortunate to be able to understand that phrase on a very personal level. I offer this collection of stories in the hope that you can catch a glimpse of what I saw.

Who We Are Now

The idea that there's any sort of global leadership body that would come together to think about pandemics was both a fundamental flaw of the simulation as well as a stark illustration of the real problem—that no such global body exists.

Gabrielle

Pandemic Response Researcher

In October of 2019, I attended a simulation of a hypothetical coronavirus pandemic. In the simulation, the Global Pandemics Council convened to talk about how to handle the outbreak. The simulation was extremely well done, except that there is, in fact, no Global Pandemics Council. The idea that there's any sort of global leadership body that would come together to think about pandemics was both a fundamental flaw of the simulation as well as a stark illustration of the real problem—that no such global body exists.

A couple days later, I wrote a blog about the session. As I was writing and looking back through my notes, I remember thinking, *Gosh, this representative from the airline industry talked about how global travel would be disrupted and the massive impact this would have on the airline industry and then on the GDP.* But the number he used was so high it wasn't believable, so I opted not to include the number in the blog.

I have spent the past five years trying to raise awareness about pandemic preparedness, and without too much success. A colleague of mine, Carolyn, and I had hosted a monthly informal working group to talk about policy issues related to pandemic preparedness. There was always so much to talk about and so much to do, but whenever we talked to funders, no one was interested in supporting this work.

I went into 2020 continuing to talk about how a global pandemic was likely to come in our lifetime. What I realized later is that I had assumed "in my lifetime" to be a distant point in my life. And even though I had been working to raise awareness about pandemic pre-paredness for the past five years, and we had regularly talked about the impact of a pandemic on the global economy, I never thought about what it could do to my family, my neighbors, or the small businesses around my city.

It will not surprise you that the airline representative's number I thought was too high to be believable was just a tiny fraction of the massive economic impact of the COVID-19 pandemic.

Washington
May 2021

If it doesn't get better in ten minutes, I have to go to the hospital.

Zeev

New York City Resident with COVID-19

No sound on the street, no cars allowed. The only thing you heard was sirens. Ten an hour, all hours of the day. A siren in the middle of the night can only mean one thing, right? It doesn't mean that Timmy broke his foot. It means somebody's going to the hospital for COVID. You're imagining every siren is a neighbor, a friend, a loved one that's going to the hospital with an unknown chance of survival. It was relentless. The sirens were constant. It was just very vivid, you know?

You're lying in bed not feeling well, and you think, *Am I the next siren? Am I the next phone call?* Every hour that goes by, you're getting worse, not better. You read the news, you hear sirens, you look in the mirror and see how your body's reacting. The realization that *This is real. I am not doing well.*

My lungs were just unable to breathe. At least four or five times over two weeks, I literally dialed 911 and was like, *If it doesn't get better in ten minutes, I have to go to the hospital.*

New York
December 2020

*Were we going to be shaking hands? Were we
going to be hugging people?*

Cathy

Charity Golf Tournament Host

The annual charity golf tournament for St. Jude
Children's Research Hospital was scheduled for March 5 through 8.

As we got closer to the date and there was more and more in the
news about the virus, we started having conversations we never expected. Were we going to be shaking hands? Were we going to be
hugging people? There's always a lot of both going on during those
four days. It was very strange to even have to think about not doing
something that is so natural, something we all do instinctively.

We always open the golf tournament with the Songwriters' Night,
and my husband, Patrick, gets up onstage to welcome everyone. So
Patrick got up there and said, basically, "I know we've got this thing
on the horizon and everybody wants to deal with it in a different way.
Some people are not comfortable shaking hands. I'm going to be just
fist-bumping. I hope you're not offended, just trying to be safe." My
resolve to be safe quickly dissipated because once you start having social cocktails with people, I kind of had the attitude of like, "It's fine."
Patrick, however, continued to be safe.

A couple days after the tournament wrapped up, we were hanging
out in our hotel room, and I turned on the local news just in time to
hear that Coachella and Stagecoach were canceling their April festivals.
Both of those happen in Palm Desert, just like our tournament.

Patrick and I were stunned. We were grateful that we got to have the
tournament and raise money for St. Jude's, but we were also thinking,
*When we get back home, we need to quarantine because look at how many
people we have been around.* We thought for sure we were going to get
it or that somebody at the tournament was going to have turned up

and had it. But as it ended up happening, we didn't get it and we aren't aware of anyone who got it.

I guess that would be considered a "St. Jude moment." That's what they call it when something extraordinary happens that they can't really put their finger on, and they attribute that to maybe St. Jude looking down on them because they're doing something good.

California
August 2021

··

Do we have the Indianapolis 500 as a television
show or do we just postpone it?

Curt

INDYCAR Writer

INDYCAR was planning to start the 2020 season
with a street race in St. Petersburg, Florida, on the weekend of March
13–15. The traveling circus, as I like to call the sport, arrived in St. Pete
at various times ahead of the first practice. Some of us were on a plane
the night before, some of us were on a plane that morning, some of us
were driving to the event. The point is, we were scattered as important
decisions were being made, and we were all racing to catch up to the
developments.

We were prepared to go racing with a crowd probably of 50,000
people in downtown St. Pete along the waterfront. Then we started
getting word of issues related to what we now know in our vernacular
as "the pandemic."

Then that day, the twelfth, the NCAA announced it was canceling its
national tournament. That was really a head-scratcher for me. I didn't
understand why it would be a problem for basketball players who had
been around each other, you know, for nine months. But at the time
we didn't have enough scope to comprehend it properly.

INDYCAR competitors don't interact like basketball players, who
lean and sweat on each other and who breathe in each other's faces.
They are race car drivers who are in their single cars, and the crews
are largely separated by distance anyway. And our fans are outside, not
in a closed-in arena.

So at first we thought, "Well, we can still stage this race, we're an
outdoor event. We can continue to be around each other when we're
outside, so there's no need to worry." It wasn't until much later that we
all learned about hotspots.

Then we started thinking that maybe we could still have the race but just not accept spectators. We already had all the TV components set up, so we could still have the race and televise it. Again, our competitors are generally socially distanced by virtue of being around their own cars and wearing all of the safety equipment (helmets, fireproof uniforms, etc.).

It became pretty clear, though, within the first few hours of deliberation and executives meeting, that we as a sport couldn't hold even an outdoor event in the middle of March in 2020. What that did was create a ripple effect through the sports world.

We were scheduled to have seventeen events during the course of the year, including the 104th edition of the Indianapolis 500, which was set for May 30. All those events in March, April, and May were either canceled or pushed back to later in the 2020 calendar. What ended up happening was we started the season in June and we pushed the Indianapolis 500 to August 22, which gave us more time to understand the ramifications of the pandemic and to adjust accordingly. Instead of doing seventeen races in 2020, we were able to stage fourteen because some of them dropped off the calendar. It was just impossible, for example, to hold races in California during that period.

At any rate, we scheduled the Indianapolis 500 on August 22 with the hope that we could still have fans attending. Typically, we have more than 300,000 people attending the race, and they come from all fifty states and all over the world.

But how do you bring 300,000 spectators into a facility even as large as Indianapolis Motor Speedway? We have sixteen gates, four or five tunnels, an enormous amount of property. And you're bringing people from all different directions in high volume. How do you test them? How do you provide sanitizer? How do you provide masks? How do you properly space them? The number of logistics to consider is just incredible, but the staff soldiered on with various plans for numerous possibilities.

It became clear as mid-July arrived that we still couldn't hold the 500 with fans in spite of our tremendous efforts to socially distance the grandstands, to make proper arrangements for sanitation, to provide masks, and so forth. So all that work in June and July essentially just had to be shelved.

Then we had to make the decision: Do we have the Indianapolis 500 as a television show or do we just postpone it? Given the importance of the Super Bowl of open-wheel racing being held and the ramifications of it not being held, we made the decision that the race must go on, and the show must go on. We held the Indianapolis 500 in a theater, if you will, with NBC delivering a terrific live show hosted by Mike Tirico. For the first time in its history, the Indianapolis 500 was held in the Indianapolis Motor Speedway without fans in the grandstands.

It was a very hollow environment. The race is normally very colorful when you put 300,000 people packing the grandstands, the infield, in various suites, and so forth. And in this particular case, much like our world in general, the race was very gray, based on the color of those grandstand seats. So we ran an Indy 500 without spectators, but our fans were still connected through television. It became a pretty good show, as good a show as you can put on in an empty arena.

We continued the season and eventually found something of a rhythm as a television product. We did the best we could, just like most sports entities that were severely impacted.

We made it through. We are fortunate to have an owner of Indianapolis Motor Speedway and the NTT INDYCAR SERIES—Roger Penske—who is a brilliant man with vast resources and a diversified company, and that allowed us to weather the storm. I think had we not had the strength and the depth of resources that Penske Corporation provides, we might not have exited the pandemic, or survived the pandemic, as well as we did.

Indiana
April 2021

Sue

Las Vegas Tourist

My friend's daughter turned eighteen on March 17 and my present to her was a big birthday celebration in Las Vegas. She had never been to Vegas, and I thought she would have the time of her life, a birthday she'd never forget. Well, she'll never forget it, that's for sure.

I picked her up from the airport on March 17. On the way to our hotel at Treasure Island, her mom called and said, "You need to show her this hotel and that hotel and the beautiful fountains here." I said, "Of course!"

When we got to the hotel, there was a skeleton staff at the desk. They said, "Vegas is shutting down at six, they just made the decision." And I said, "How do you shut down Vegas?"

I asked the gal, "Are we going to be kicked out of our rooms?" She said, "No, but everything's going to be closed." I said, "Well, what about food?" She said, "I don't know."

All I knew was that it was about four o'clock and I had to get my friend's daughter to all these hotels before they closed at six. So we ran from hotel to hotel, and every time we got to a hotel, they were shutting their doors, they were closing early. Then I said, "You've got to see these fountains," so we ran over there only to find that the fountains were off. We dashed off to see the Forum Shops at Caesars Palace, but all of them were closing their doors and locking up. I had never seen anything like this. I was just mystified.

Next up was food. We went back to our hotel, hoping the restaurant would be open. When we got there, there were no other patrons, just us. All of the waitstaff were milling around the bar. Finally we waved a waitress down and she came over to us very unenthusiastically. I asked, "What's happening?" She said, "We all lost our jobs today." She had a tear in her eye and clearly had been crying. I felt badly for her. I said, "I'm so sorry."

She replied, "Yeah, I have two kids and I don't know how I'm going to feed them. I'm a single mom. I don't even know if I can get a job or if any of us can get jobs. Everybody in Vegas is reliant upon their jobs in the hospitality industry." She was so upset, she was just beside herself.

I told her we wanted to get something to eat because we didn't know the next time we'd be able to find an open place. So we ate some dinner and I said to my friend's daughter, "Let's go to the game floor. I just want to play some slots before everything is closed." She stood at the entrance, because of her age, and I went over to the slots. All of a sudden, the entire row of slots turned dark. And they went in succession, with one row after the other going dark. I never got to put any money in a machine because every time I went to a machine, it was that row that was going dark.

It was the weirdest experience I've ever had in Vegas. Seeing it shut down was so strange. When we went back to the room, I called my friend and said, "This may not be a great eighteenth birthday, but I'll tell you what, she'll never forget it. It's going to make history."

Our room was huge, a suite on a top floor. It was like only forty bucks because there was nobody staying at the hotel, and it was the last night. Around sunset, we went to the window and saw the sun go down and then the lights went out in Vegas. There were no cars on the street. There were no lights on the hotels. I was just shocked and sad. How many times is Vegas going to go dark? They have shows that go dark, but not Vegas.

Nevada
March 2021

Do not lock me up in my house.

Amy

Wife and Mother

All of a sudden our schools shut down and my work is telling us to stay home. All of the restaurants, bars, everything, close down. I literally remember sitting at my house in a daze, looking into space, going, "What has happened?"

It was the most horrible feeling because I am a people person. Do not lock me up in my house and tell me I can't go anywhere for a month. I will go crazy, especially with my husband and my children there all the time. Before COVID, my husband was on the road three weeks out of every month and now he's been home since last March; he hasn't traveled. It's been so crazy and hectic in our household. I became the teacher, the lunch lady, the dazed and confused grocery-washing, fruit-washing lunatic. When I first went out, I had such bad anxiety, just making a trip to, like, Sam's to get necessities. I would be like, "Oh my gosh, we're going to get the virus." It was terrifying, not knowing.

I think I cried every day. You know why? Because there was no end in sight. Usually I know how long something is going to last. "Okay, we have to do this until this time." Not with this. It was, "Well, maybe this summer, you know, things will go back to normal," and then "Oh, no, nothing is back to normal." It was very chaotic; I had to learn to adapt. We have adapted to the "new normal," but I don't like the new normal. I don't. I can't wait for it to go back to the way it used to be. I hate when people say, "Well, it's the new normal." No, no, no, no, no. I refuse. Let's get back to *normal*. I want to get back to that, but that means getting vaccinated and taking precautions. Let's go back to where we can gather as a crowd—you know, the good old United States like when I grew up as a kid. I want that.

North Dakota
February 2021

*Healthcare people, we just keep going. We have a
duty to report, so we just go.*

Linda

ER Nurse

In February, I got sick after coming back from a
friend's wedding in Florida. I had a lingering cough for a week or two
and then I started getting sicker and sicker. I tried to get a COVID test,
but the Department of Health wouldn't approve it because I hadn't
traveled outside the United States. They would not test me even though
I was an ER nurse. I ended up getting some intermittent fevers. It was
strange because I would get up, thinking I felt okay, and then I would
get really faint and have to lie back down. I did that for about three days.
Then I went back to work. Healthcare people, we just keep going. We
have a duty to report, so we just go.

The ER was a mess. Our infection-control protocols were developing and changing every day, and we didn't know if we were protected. It
was scary and overwhelming. We started looking at everyone like they
were potentially contagious, and that changed how we approached our
patients. We were scared of them, which isn't really a normal feeling.
When a patient would come in, we would isolate them immediately.
Then one nurse would be responsible for treating that patient and be
gowned up completely. No one else would go in the room, and you'd
talk to the patient on a phone, looking at them through the door window, just like in the *Contagion*-type movies.

The patients kept adding up, and soon there were so many patients
that you could not separate anyone. We had carts with the PPE [per-
sonal protective equipment] for infection control, but there weren't
enough carts. You'd be running all over and everyone's yelling, and you
can't hear anybody when you're all masked and gowned, and then we're
intubating everyone, which is scary when it's spewing all this stuff.

At that time, we were trying to get a lot of information from Italy, learning from them, because China really wasn't sharing their story. We'd see all those people's stories and interviews from Italy, and I remember feeling like we could see our future. Yet there were so many people around me that didn't take it seriously. That was difficult for me. I just kind of withdrew and just did my job. When I wasn't at work, I didn't want to talk about it. It was overwhelming. I did some gardening and cooking and coloring, and I started knitting. I just did things that kind of settled me and made me feel content and helped me recharge so I could go back in and do it again.

The support from family and friends and people I didn't even know was honestly one of the most beautiful things I've probably ever experienced. People were sending cards and food and all kinds of support to us at the hospital, and I personally was getting packages from people across the country. Homemade masks and gloves with notes saying, "You need these more than we do." That was so touching. My neighbor's son, who works at a local produce store, brought over a little orchid-type plant and said, "Thank you so much for everything." It was all humbling and beautiful.

Illinois
February 2021

*I didn't intend to become an Overlord. This
whole effort just grew like crazy over the course of
ten days.*

Kristina

Comedian and Founder of the Auntie Sewing Squad

It's kind of a wild story, how I went from come-
dian to Overlord of the Auntie Sewing Squad, a nationwide sweatshop
of volunteers who made and delivered 250,000 face masks. This was
not how I expected my 2020 to go. I have these moments where I'm
just like, *How did I get in so deep?* Like, literally my first mask was sewn
on a Hello Kitty sewing machine.

I'm a performance artist, comedian, and a local elected representative in my neighborhood of Koreatown, Los Angeles. I wrote a show
about it called *Kristina Wong for Public Office* and had a national tour
set in cities all over the country. It was going to run alongside all the
real-life rallies and events leading up to November's election. That was
supposed to be my 2020. I premiered the show in February in Los
Angeles, and it was the greatest show of my life. The standing ovation
started even before the show was over. It truly was the greatest show
of my life. And something that I could not imagine doing without an
audience. I did one more show in March at a community college in
Sacramento, and basically twenty minutes before I finished the show,
all the students got a text saying, "We're going online tomorrow." And
then the show the next day in Santa Cruz was canceled.

It was really kind of a perilous, scary drive back to Los Angeles,
where I live, because the big question was "How am I going to make
a living as an artist who tours live if I can't be in front of crowds?"
And I thought, *Maybe this will just be a month, we'll just lock down for a
month.* But within a week, I was like, *There's got to be something I can
do rather than just watch the news and be horrified and do nothing.* Then

I saw that hospitals were asking for homemade masks. And I was like, *Oh, I have an essential skill even though I'm not an essential worker.* So I used the pattern I saw online and took some scraps of elastic and fabric that I happened to have in the house. I sewed my first mask and very naively offered it to the world. "If you're immunocompromised or have no access to a mask, let me make you a mask. You can just reimburse me for shipping and, if you don't even have that, don't worry about it." That ballooned very quickly in the course of four days into hundreds of requests. It was very hard to say no. It was very hard to say, "I'm sorry, I have limits." These people were putting themselves at risk to keep the world going, and what am I going to say, "I'm sorry, I got in over my head"?

I got a neighbor, Audrey, to help me cut fabric. I was saying to Audrey and my other friends, "I can't believe it's people, just people like us, who are going to save us at this moment. It's so weird." Now there are teams of Aunties all over who are doing this labor. I love this image of an auntie. When I'm called an auntie by little kids and I'm not actually their biological aunt, my heart just warms. It's a very sweet way, especially in Asian communities, to refer to elder women. So I called the group the Auntie Sewing Squad.

The whole sweatshop Overlord persona I take on is because our first volunteers were all Asian American women and it was just sort of a joke. I was like, "What's happening? What kind of weird ancestral destiny is this? It's turning into a Chinese sweatshop, that's what's happening!" And so it's funny because now our group has lots of different kinds of women—white women, Asian, Black, Latinx, and some Indigenous women. They all call me the Overlord, and it all stems from this Chinese sweatshop reference.

I didn't intend to become an overlord. This whole effort just grew like crazy over the course of ten days. It went from me gathering this group to me suddenly facilitating donations from interior designers and people who just had rolls of fabric lying around and then getting them out to other people and then tutoring people on the phone on how to use their sewing machine because they hadn't touched it in a while.

We're not just like ladies who love quilting. This has been exhausting. It's been hard. We are people who are just horrified watching vulnerable communities faced with fatalities from this virus when there are basic protections in the form of cloth and elastic that can keep them from getting sick. It seems very logical to me that if we keep them safe, we keep us safe. Your health is my health. That's what this is. That's what this pandemic could have been—a moment to really realize how interconnected we are. Instead, it became this weird partisan thing, which has had devastating consequences.

I don't want to preserve this pandemic. I don't want to preserve this level of work, but this level of connection that we've made with each other as total strangers, the love and care that we express for each other and for other communities, I would love to see that continue beyond this time. Not necessarily at this level of hellish work, but it has opened my heart in this way. I think if anyone is out there watching this and they've been feeling scared and helpless, I think the answer is to figure out how to give. That may sound counterintuitive, like if you are facing job scarcity or you're not even sure where your next meal is coming from, how to figure out how you can be generous. A lot of our Aunties are not employed and they're dealing with their own losses. Sewing gives them a sense of purpose. You have to have a purpose; you have to have something that gets you up in the morning.

My dream is that when this is over, all the Aunties from the different cities will come together. I really hope that's how this ends, that we retire from making masks. Then I'll go on tour with my new show, *Kristina Wong, Sweatshop Overlord*. It unfolds across the pandemic, playing out mostly here in my house. It chronicles what it has been like to run the sewing group, with no experience whatsoever, from my home, during a pandemic like none of us have ever seen. How I experienced the pandemic seems to be very interesting to people who have not run a national sweatshop out of their house.

California
December 2020

There was no playbook for us mayors to turn to.
We had to figure it out in real time.

Cedric

Mayor

I'm in my second year of my first term as mayor of Forrest City, so there was a lot for me to learn even before the pandemic struck. When it first hit the U.S. in areas like New York, I figured it was going to be about three or four weeks before it affected us down here in Arkansas. We spent that time preparing, knowing it could completely overwhelm our healthcare system. There was no playbook for us mayors to turn to. We had to figure it out in real time.

I realized one of the big issues in our area was communication, especially on the local level. In our rural community, many people still read the local newspaper, listen to the radio talk shows, and follow community events on social media. The biggest issue was how to reach the most vulnerable members of our community, the elderly, the low-income individuals, and people with special needs. That most vulnerable portion of our community still can only be reached door to door or through something that comes into their mailboxes. Everyone gets a water bill, so we would do inserts that contained information about COVID and flattening the curve. It was important for this information to come from trusted sources.

One of our key messages has been "Pay attention to what's happening locally." I was on the radio two or three times a week, in the newspaper once a week, and on social media, just making sure the messages came from here and addressed local needs. Because if you turn on the TV, everything is politicized so much that you have people in a panic. So the key was continuing to keep the communication lines open from local leadership about what's happening locally.

In the beginning, the focus was to flatten the curve, because we figured this thing was getting ready to come in and wipe everything out. But what we saw transforming was that people were starting to do business and go about their days in a different way. So the curve was flattened. And I truly believe that because of the work of our leadership between the city, county, school district, and our local task force, it wasn't as bad when it got here. People were really taking a lot of precautions and we did a lot of testing. I mean, currently—and I'm going to just knock on wood—we're still in single digits of deaths here in St. Francis County. And that's truly a blessing, especially with the federal prison in our county.

But this is not a sprint. It's going to be a marathon, and we're just going to have to learn how to continue to live our lives, but live it in a safe manner.

We have been working together as a community, all hands on deck, to get through it. That's one of the beautiful things about rural communities like Forrest City. When times are tough, we find a way to get it done and we pull together and help each other. Our local newspaper and some businesses even teamed up to put signs all over town saying "We're All in This Together." And that's what we're doing in this unique 2020.

Arkansas
October 2020

They felt isolated, and that's hard. Kids need each other.

Cindy

Teacher

I know the day well, Friday the thirteenth. We thought Friday the thirteenth with a full moon was going to be a tough day for us, especially with special ed. Little did we know that we were going to be told that we had to leave the building for two weeks.

During those two weeks, we really kind of had time off. We were not engaged in instruction. And, of course, I immediately wanted to reach out to people to say, "What can I do to help?" I went to my mom's and helped her do things around her house. I went to the school garden, which I've been a part of now for a number of years. I was just waiting for the two weeks to end and then for us to begin again, right?

Then we were told, "We are going to now be learning and teaching online, and this is how we're going to do it. We are going to start on this date, but we're going to have a week to try it out with just the teachers and without the kids."

I panicked; it was a lot of new technology that I had not seen before. We went with the Google platform, Google Classroom, Google Meet, and Google Chat. I had to learn all of that. I did have a laptop, but it wasn't the most high-tech laptop. I thought I had to buy a new piece of equipment or at least borrow something that's better than what I had, which I was able to do, luckily. It was a big learning curve to figure out how to use the new technology and then to see how we were going to implement it in terms of what reading programs we were using and what lessons were going to look like: *Is it still going to be in our regular curriculum that we can access, or is it all going to be modified now because we're doing it differently?*

Then we began teaching. It was interactive to a certain point, but there was a lot of work that was done independently. I would go in and read the assignments and pull out kids individually to say, "Let's take a look at this. How are you going to approach it? How are you going to respond to the questions in this story?" It was very difficult to try to navigate with the kids, who were also new to the technology, although they're much quicker learners than us adults.

The biggest challenge was that not everybody had laptops and Chromebooks. We had families that had multiple kids in a family, four or five kids. Did they have a laptop for everybody? No. So we had to survey how many children were without technology, who needed technology. We had to realize that there are kids who live in two different homes—they might be with Dad for a couple, three days, and we had to hope that they remembered to take their laptops to Mom's. So there were many challenges along the way; not everybody had what they needed.

I had a number of kids who weren't even showing up. We had to email them, we had to call them. We learned that they couldn't operate their Chromebook, it wasn't working, or they didn't know how to work it. We had to go through all of those glitches and problem solve.

One of the other challenges was providing meals to kids. We scheduled a break without instruction between 11 a.m. and 1 p.m. when families could go to the school to pick up meals, because we have free and reduced lunches for kids. I work with a lot of those children. I was worried: "Did you eat today? Did you get breakfast? Did you get lunch? Do you know that you can go to the school and get meals provided?" Mom and Dad worked, or older siblings were at home but didn't drive, so we had those issues too.

We have a lot of kids who speak English as a second language. Those kids were really struggling, because it was those families that were out the door working every day, and it was up to their siblings to help run the show. A lot of responsibility fell on older siblings, but they had their studies to do too. It was very interesting to see how families operated in this whole change. Some worked better than others. I found myself reaching out to a lot more kids. I wasn't going to let them, you know, scramble along the way.

A month to six weeks later, we were kind of finally settled in and were able to create a schedule. Our year was over around the third week of June, and it had all felt very disjointed at first, but I felt like we got into a nice routine with the proper structure. We were able to provide the courses and communicate with other teachers about what was and wasn't working. We evaluated from week to week. How many children were showing up, how many were not—that way we could reach out to those families. By week six or seven, we were at about 90-something percent for having children in the virtual classroom.

We're a school that's pretty family strong, and we're very fortunate that the families are engaged and that they're involved for the most part. There are a lot of other schools in the county that are not like that, so I feel grateful that I'm at a school where there is parent support.

It was hard because we were all missing seeing the kids, we were missing that interaction, and we were missing each other, being together as a staff. I think the hardest part was the lack of human connection. As a teacher, that's a big part of what you do every day. Greetings and hugs of comfort. We can't read a kid's body language very well through a computer. You don't know what's really going on, how the kids are truly feeling. In my Google Meets, I would try to bring some of that personal touch into the conversation, because that is what's really lacking. I could see the look on some of these kids' faces, and they were miserable. They missed their friends, they missed their peers. They weren't doing their sports programs, they weren't in any of the clubs that we have before school and after school. They felt isolated, and that's hard. Kids need each other.

Maryland
November 2020

*We "locked in" with our members and we kept
the world out. We kept coronavirus out.*

Donna

Senior Living Community Executive

The coronavirus came to our campus on March
13. It was one employee and we sent them home. I then went to my
boss, the CEO of our company, and said, "Our best strategy right now
is to lock in. We'll ask employees to volunteer to live on campus and
we'll reward them. And we will just live on campus with our members.
It'll be over in two weeks, four weeks max." He never blinked. He was
behind me 100 percent.

We didn't call it "lock out." We "locked in" with our members and
we kept the world out. We kept coronavirus out. The gate was literally
locked, and the only thing that came in and out of that gate was food
deliveries, Amazon packages, and Instacart.

I asked for volunteers from our employee body, and sixty people
raised their hands immediately.

They included our director of accounting, our moving coordinator,
servers, housekeepers, maintenance, security. I took any volunteer
who raised their hand. Ended up being seventy-five. The next step was
figuring out where people were going to sleep, how we were going to
feed employees, and how we were going to keep the operations of our
500-member community running with a staff of seventy-five instead
of 300.

Some of the employees lived in model rooms, some lived in rooms
on air mattresses, and some people, like me, lived in our health center,
with memory care and skilled nursing. I lived in a tent in the community hall.

We left our titles at the door and we all took on different roles, whatever we needed to do to take care of members. Everybody at mealtime

became someone that delivered meals. Everyone became someone who would disinfect our common areas. Everyone became whatever we needed them to be in the moment. I don't even know that some of my employees that I was serving with knew I was the COO. They just knew I was that girl that came and made French toast on Sunday mornings and vacuumed the hallways and helped do laundry. It didn't matter because it was all of us together, fighting a common enemy called COVID.

Each day, I would crawl out of my tent, put on my scrubs and ball cap, and go down to see who needed help with breakfast. I might be feeding a member, I might be cooking in the kitchen, I might be just engaging with members around a game of cards or a board game, or painting nails or giving a haircut. By the time breakfast was over, it was already lunchtime, and we were making sure that everybody was eating and getting their meals. Days were filled with making sure our households were clean, members' rooms were clean, laundry was done for everyone, and everyone received their medications. And spending time together, like sitting outside in the courtyard, soaking up the sun, talking and visiting. We did things to keep people entertained, too, like Zoom karaoke. They got such a hoot out of hearing me sing not well.

We were working twelve, fourteen, sixteen hours a day, doing what was needed and trying to keep everyone's spirits up. It was constant motion. I will admit that sometimes it was nice to retreat to my tent and just turn off the device and just be. I have an Energizer Bunny in my body, so it wasn't so much physically exhausting as much as just mentally exhausting. Retreating to my tent and just being by myself was a relief for me.

Two weeks went by and the coronavirus was a hot-fire mess in Georgia. Then four weeks. I got everyone together and said, "If you need to go home, you can. You did what I asked you to do. You committed for four weeks. But I still need you." That's the hardest thing I've ever had to do as a leader, to say, "You have given me what you promised, but I need more." And every time I did that, they would say, "You can count on me." And that's not about me, it's about what we do here. It's about our mission of loving and serving members. We make a promise to them that they never have to leave, that we will move them through the continuum of care as they progress in age, and that we will always take care of them.

This was a wonderful example of seeing people living our mission in action. It was about living it to the extreme. And it was a beautiful thing. Our employees talk about our members as their second family. We got to live that; we got to see it in action.

Employees made a commitment to leave their own families during this crisis so they could take care of the members of their second family. We have one director of nursing who has six kids, a husband, and her mom who lives with them. She talked to her family, and she said, "I feel like I need to do this." And the family said, "Don't worry about us. You go and do this and we will take care of home." I've got a picture of her standing in a window, looking at her family two stories down, waving up at the window. That's powerful commitment.

Growing up, my father was a soldier who went to Vietnam twice. You know, I was watching my father go off and hoping he would come back. With COVID, we knew we could lose members. If we didn't do extreme things like locking in, we could lose members, and we weren't willing to do that. That's what I learned from my father about mission and commitment.

We locked in for seventy-five days. When we did leave, it was because we had the processes in place, the PPE and testing in place, that we needed to make sure we could take care of our members and employees. But it was so interesting on that last day when everyone was leaving, and their families were meeting them in the parking lot. They all hung out in the parking lot talking, like they didn't quite know how to leave. They were a big family of seventy-three sisters and two brothers, needing to leave each other so they could be with their own families.

I was remembering that the other day when we finally were able to open up to family visits for our members. They had not seen their families in person, to be able to touch and hug each other, for over a year. Our staff, because they remember how emotional they were after the seventy-five days, were standing by the doors, crying, while the families were reuniting in the rooms. They knew.

We all walked away changed. You can't go through something like that and not be changed.

Georgia
July 2021

I'm going to Haiti. I'm going to get my daughter.

Carine

New Adoptive Parent

I've been in the process of adopting for over five years, and I got matched with a six-year-old last year. In January, I was really hoping that she would be able to come home. Then the adoption was delayed until February. COVID happened, and things started revving up in March. I was just like, *If there's one more delay in this adoption, things are just going to go really left.*

In early March, a friend of mine and I were in the chapel where I work, and I felt in my spirit, "Go and get your daughter." Just like that. I called my agency, because when you're doing international adoption, you have to have an agency here and you have to have an agency rep abroad. Every time I would talk to my agency rep, he or she would say "No, we don't suggest you go until all the paperwork is in order because if you go, you might get stuck and not be able to bring her."

Immediately after I left the chapel, I called the agency and said, "I'm going to Haiti. I'm going to get my daughter. I'm buying the ticket tomorrow and I want to be home by next Thursday." She said, "Well, I can't tell you not to go. We'll try to get everything done, but there's no guarantee she'll be able to come home with you." I thought, *Well, if I can't come home next Thursday, I'm going to stay for as long as it takes.*

My nephew agreed to go with me, and we flew out on Monday. We needed four things to happen while we were in Haiti for this adoption: we needed the U.S. embassy to give her a final exit; we needed her visa to be approved; we needed to get her final exit letter; and we needed her medical records to be released. And we needed it fast. New York was shutting down.

I'm telling you, it was like a miracle. All those things had to happen in sequence—and they did.

On Thursday morning, we got on the plane and came home to New Jersey. On Saturday, the State of New Jersey declared the entire state shut down.

As soon as we got home, people called saying, "You need to go and get food, there's going to be a food shortage. There's no toilet paper anywhere." The excitement of having her home was overshadowed by COVID. I went out and spent so much money on food because I had no idea what she liked, because this was a new child coming into my home. I bought everything I could think of, and we just, we were isolated. Our lives have been cocooning, you know, quarantine cocooning, since then.

The upside was that I was able to get this precious time with her by myself. But in my head, I'd had this image of all these external stimuli that would help make the transition fun and settle her into her new family and community. We would go to the zoo, we would go to the library, we would visit family and friends. She would have playdates and she would start school. Let me emphasize again, she would start school.

None of that happened.

We established a routine where we would go to the park and play, you know, and go on the swings. But then they started shutting down the playground; swings were not safe, you couldn't touch anything. Instead, we would go for a walk, but it was cold and she wasn't used to it.

So we would try to do things in the backyard. I spent tons of money on my backyard. I put the fence around there and added plants and gardens and swings, all kinds of things. I was like, *If we're going to be home and isolated, I at least need to have a safe place and a fun place.* We needed a haven so that we could have the space and the time to just be together.

The downside was that this extended amount of time, of just my daughter and myself, was very hard, and it was hard explaining it to her. The new normal. I remember one time we were riding around and she asked, "Is the whole United States shut down, Mama?" And I said, "Yeah, pretty much."

When she finally got to see people, she could only see half of their faces. She couldn't tell if they were smiling at her or not half the time. So she's come into this new normal, which unfortunately is her normal.

"Don't touch this because of COVID; don't do that because of COVID." Our nightly prayers are "Please heal the land from COVID. Don't let anyone in our family get sick from COVID." She knows the word "COVID" extremely well.

In the summer, I enrolled her in the Goddard School, one of the only programs in the state that stayed open. She started thriving, her English picked up, and she had friends, she had community; it was no longer just her and this woman she suddenly was calling "Mama."

New Jersey
November 2020

....

The first confirmed cases of coronavirus in the
state of North Carolina were in my district.

Valerie

State Senator

On March 3, I was attending a conference in Charlotte, and I got a text message from Health and Human Services. It was, to put it mildly, surprising to get a text from DHHS out of the blue. They were alerting me that the first confirmed cases of coronavirus in the state of North Carolina were in my district. Two residents of Chatham County who had traveled to Italy had contracted the disease. I knew enough to know that this was huge and that we were on our way into something that was not going to be good. I left Charlotte that day rather than staying over the next night because I knew that if there were two cases, there certainly were more.

When I look back at 2020, coming from that point of entry into where we are now, with massive unemployment because of shutdowns, and then the blowback, the pushback, it has been very, very difficult. We knew the shutdowns were not the best thing for the economy, but having this juxtaposition of the economy versus overall healthy communities was hard. The governor was in a tough position.

And in the midst of all of that, we were waiting on the federal government to bring in aid. When people started to lose their jobs and people's rents and mortgages and car payments went into jeopardy, there was no help. And the state system was not equipped to handle the massive number of unemployment insurance claims. Before COVID, we usually had about 800 or so claims a week. Then all of a sudden, we went from 800 to 1,800 to 300,000.

Our constituents were coming to us saying, "I followed everything you told me, Senator. I filed my unemployment claim and I've waited for three weeks now. When I call, nobody answers the phone. When I

29

go online, I get knocked off. When I do stay online, I keep getting the same thing saying I'm not eligible. I know I'm eligible. I can't pay my rent and my family is going to be out on the street. Can you help me?"

How many of those folks do you think I could help? Very few. And then the small businesses were calling and saying, "Senator, we're not eligible for PPP [Paycheck Protection Program]." Or "Senator, you can only apply through certain banks or lending institutions. I've never done this before. I need technical assistance in applying." Or "Senator, I don't have an established relationship with this bank, so they will not even talk to me. So where's our help?" That's so painful.

And then I got the call that brought everything really close to home. It went like this.

"Hey, Valerie, how are you?"

"I'm good, how are you?"

"Not so good. So-and-so died of COVID."

"No, can't be."

"Yes."

"What happened?"

"Well, you know he had surgery. After the surgery, he was sent to a convalescent center. He contracted COVID there and died in four days."

Two days later, his family asked me if I would eulogize him. The ceremony was on May 2. There was no church service, just a graveside service, because of course we had to be outside. Afterwards, my husband and I just drove around because I just was not ready to go inside. While we were driving, I got a phone call. I had noticed at the funeral that my friend's best friend was not there. Well, so I got the call from another friend who was at the funeral. This is how it went:

"Valerie, I know this is going to upset you, but they found Kenneth dead today."

"What do you mean?"

"That's why he wasn't at the funeral."

He was only two years older than me. Kenneth was the editor and publisher of the *Carolina Times* newspaper, one of the few Black newspapers in our state. So that's no more. That's the end of an era that started with his grandfather, Louis Austin, way back in 1927.

And so, when I quiet myself, those are the things I most vividly remember.

North Carolina
December 2020

Frank

COVID-19 Ventilator Patient

I was working for a nonprofit organization driving a bus. We would bring older people, people on Medicare, back and forth to doctor appointments, rehab centers. I come home from work, sit down, and watch TV, and all of a sudden, I can't breathe. I called my son and he took me to the hospital. They diagnosed me: "You have COVID." I said, "Man, I ain't got no COVID."

The next morning, Dr. M. come and say, "What's the matter?" I'm telling him I come here last night, and the doctor told me I have COVID. I just couldn't breathe. He said, "Are you ready to go home?" I said, "Yeah." So they let me come home. Got home, next day, the same thing. Can't breathe.

They had an ambulance service come get me. They came in here and gave me a breathing treatment and took me to the hospital. And when I got there, on March 24, Dr. M. say he's going to put me in a medically induced coma. I went to sleep on March 24 and when I woke up, it was April 23. I'd been on a ventilator for almost thirty days. The hospital's head of infectious medicine told Dr. M. to unplug me earlier than that, but Dr. M. said, "Man, I'm in the business of saving lives. I'm not going to unplug that man and tell his family he is brain dead, which he's not."

When I woke up, I asked my wife when was Easter, and she said, "Boy, Easter been gone." And I say, "Where I been?" And she said, "You been out, asleep." But I didn't remember nothing, and I didn't realize how sick I was until I called my wife and said, "When you come get me?" and she said, "Not right now." I had no idea that I couldn't walk. I had no idea. I couldn't go to the bathroom. I couldn't pull up in the bed. I couldn't use nothing on my body. Hands, legs, feet, nothing. I couldn't do nothing, period, in a vegetative state. I lost the use of everything, man.

They told me they would send me to a rehab center. When I got there, they put me in a room, and the next thing I know, they put me on a second floor by myself and told me that I got COVID again. So I stayed thirty days in there, with everybody masked up, aproned up, gloved up. And they just got me laying there in the bed, can't turn over, can't feed myself, can't do nothing. And nobody could come visit me because I was in isolation.

Every time they come in the room, they'd say, "Why are you down in that hole?" "Man, I've been trying to get out of this hole, but I don't have the strength to pull myself up." And then they get mad with you, they'd bring three or four people in and take you out of the hole and then all of a sudden you're back in that hole. Yeah, I mean, I'm laying flat like this for three months. It was supposed to be a rehab center, but they did nothing for me.

I finally got out of there and back to the hospital to do rehab. In two weeks, I was able to stand at the parallel bars and sit in this wheelchair and push up. And then they started walking me, and it was amazing because I hadn't walked in ninety-something days. I got off-balance and never could get the strength. I would walk with a walker and then I would get tired. Like right now, I still get tired fast, I still don't have no balance, still can't taste every now and then, still can't smell every now and then.

I know there's a God 'cause it's a miracle that I am here. The guy's son who does the dialysis tell me, "Mr. Frank, you're a walking miracle." I say, "What are you talking about?" He say, "Frankie, everyone who was on that floor that had COVID, all of them died but you." And he say, "I know there is a God, you blessed."

Then Dr. V., the heart doctor, say, "Man, we really thought you was going to die." Dr. S., "Man, we really thought you was going to die." You know, it's a bad feeling when everybody coming to you, telling you that they really thought you was going to die. And they look at you, "Man, Frank!" and you don't remember.

The doctor told me maybe it's good I don't remember. You know? And I'll be asking my wife, "What happened?" And she'll be telling me, and I don't remember. He said, "That's a part of your life that you will never be able to get back." That's fine, I'm here now. I don't wish this on nobody, man.

Louisiana
January 2021

It felt like a war room. It felt like disaster planning.

Sara

Critical Care Physician

When the first case was announced in Washington State, I think many of us figured if it's already in Washington, it's probably been circulating in the community and we just didn't know it. We weren't testing, so no one had any idea. And I remember, reflecting back to winter 2019, we were seeing a lot of cases of viral pneumonia in the hospital on the ventilator. We would run our viral panels and they were all negative. Patients were really sick and dying, and I think many of us question, in retrospect, whether it was here before we actually knew it.

Once the planning started, it was extremely rapid. It felt like a war room. It felt like disaster planning. And while we were going through the motions, I think there was this sense of disbelief that any of our plans would ever be needed. We have a huge intensive care unit, we're not going to run out of beds, we're not going to have to put patients in areas of the hospital that don't normally house ICU patients. But almost every single thing we accounted for happened.

The worst period of time for us was March through May of 2020. It was pretty horrific here and it came very fast. We were one of the first cities, shortly after New York, to really experience a surge, so we didn't know what we were dealing with. We didn't know how best to manage these patients and how best to treat them. That was a really uncomfortable place to be as a physician, when our training is all about knowing the right thing to do and knowing what the next steps are. There was a sense of helplessness to some degree.

Typically, in the medical world, it takes time for shifts in practice to happen, and that comes as the result of clinical trials and research published in peer-reviewed journals. They're scrutinized by the scientific community, and that can take years. We didn't have that time in this situation, so it was literally doctors posting on Twitter what they were noticing. There were physician Facebook groups where doctors were sharing their experiences, pooling resources: "I found this article" or "I spoke to this person" or "Here's what I saw" or "Are you guys seeing this?" It worked pretty well, and you had to hashtag every post with keywords so they were searchable. We organized pretty quickly.

This sharing of observations and brainstorming in terms of what could possibly help in real time is not how we are used to doing things. I think many of us would say that we tend to enjoy a little bit more certainty in our field. We typically have clear guidelines on what to do, and this was all very new and very different than anything we'd ever seen before. On the one hand, I think it was great how the scientific community came together so rapidly and in such a robust way. On the other hand, it made it even more important for us to scrutinize the information we were getting and take a hard look at it, because it wasn't what we call evidence based. It wasn't solid research. That was challenging. In the spring, we had conference calls with counterparts in Italy and China and talked to their critical care groups about what they felt worked for these patients and what didn't. We were all in the trenches, and we had to figure it out fairly quickly if we were going to have any sort of positive impact.

I think collectively there has been a lot of burnout. It's not about the work. It's not about how many hours you work or how tired everyone is. The challenge is the emotional burden that has come with this pandemic in terms of witnessing a degree of suffering that we are not accustomed to seeing. That has caused a lot of moral injury in healthcare providers across the board. Then there's the other side of things where the community does not seem to appreciate how horrific what's happening is. What do you do with that?

I'm a critical care physician, so I work in the ICU. And in the ICU, there are always going to be patients who die, who don't survive their illnesses. But it's something else to see patients dying alone, to know that their families are unable to be with them, to know that we are their last connection to the outside world. To hear patients talk to their loved ones before going on the ventilator, telling them about bank account numbers and passwords. Trying to get their family's affairs in order in the very last minute because they walked into the hospital, but things deteriorated so quickly, and they recognize that going on the ventilator probably meant they weren't going to survive. Holding phones up to patients' ears as they're dying and hearing the family members say their goodbyes. It hurts and has been devastating. And when people go around and don't wear masks, or don't believe COVID is real, or don't social-distance, it adds to that hurt even more.

Michigan
January 2021

*If this is who we're relying on—people like me—
across America to save lives, we're definitely all
going to die.*

Claudie

Massage Therapist Turned PPE Distributor

Every year has been so different for me. I didn't have expectations about what 2020 was going to be like, but it definitely wasn't going to include something as ginormous as a pandemic. I didn't even really know what a pandemic was, and I didn't want to know, to be honest. I don't want to know about UFOs, I don't want to know about asteroids, I don't want to know how big a tsunami can get because I cannot control it, and I'm a bit of a control freak.

I got sick with a temperature and a sore throat on March 10 or something like that. The next day, the WHO declared COVID-19 a pandemic. I thought maybe what I had was COVID, so I phoned the hospital. There were no tests at that point, though, so I just stayed at home and recovered. I didn't really reach out to people or friends, and I didn't spread the sick or power through it like I normally would. About two weeks later, I felt better and went down to the beach. It was really weird, everybody was sitting so far apart.

My daughter and I were alone for most of the early on. Then by about early April, I was in such a tizz that I started having literal panic attacks. My arms just started feeling weightless, my face was tingling, I shut down my frontal cortex. I couldn't speak. I was nonverbal for a couple days, which was scary. I remember trying to make my daughter an avocado sandwich and it took me an hour and a half. I couldn't control anything. I was on the edge, which was scary. It was horrible, and there was nothing I could do.

I started doing a deep dive because I was so traumatized by Donald Trump's lack of leadership that I realized we're on our own. We are literally on our own. Our community has one very, very small hospital with fourteen ICU beds, and that's it. And we're also cut off from food because we import 95 percent of our food supply here in Maui. My thoughts were, *I just have to stay alive and get through this with my daughter.* I was not mentally doing well at all.

Two of my friends who work at the hospital called me crying. A husband who is a respiratory therapist and his wife, a nurse. They were sobbing, saying, "The hospital will not allow us to wear masks in community workstations, in the elevators, or in the hallways. The only place we are allowed to wear PPE is going in and out of patient rooms." So I'm like, "Give me his email, we're going to town."

So suddenly I shifted from focusing on what I couldn't control to having a project. I called the editor of the local newspaper, and I was like, "I have a story for you. Maybe you can make this situation public and shame the hospital into allowing the staff to not only use PPE but to bring in their own PPE." After nine or so days, they reversed their decision and finally allowed the doctors and nurses to wear PPE.

Now the problem was that there wasn't enough PPE in the state of Hawaii or anywhere in the world. The editor of the paper calls me and says, "Claudie, I know this is strange and I know this isn't what you do, but I have a friend who called me frantically saying that he works for a hoverboard company in China that owns twenty factories and they're all pivoting into PPE. He's in charge of so many states and liaising with these procurement agencies that he needs someone in Hawaii who cares and doesn't have a job right now and has a computer to take over the procurement center in Honolulu and try to get PPE from these factories in China. And I think that's your calling right now."

I was like, "Okay, I don't know how to do a Google Doc, I'm a hippie massage therapist and I've been here for twenty years and everything's very manual with me." I had a computer, but I just used it for photos and emails. I didn't even know how to make an attachment to an email.

Long story short, I started working with the Honolulu procurement agency to procure PPE from China. This company was renting Boeings and flying it over here. We got a lot of bites and suddenly had a big team of, I think, fifteen people across America who each had three or four states. I had Delaware, Ohio, and Hawaii. And the jails. It was nuts.

I started realizing that I didn't know what I'm doing, but it was really important work. And it was really scary and I was thinking, *If this is who we're relying on—people like me—across America to save lives, we're definitely all going to die.*

Then I started having panic attacks again. I was picturing a tsunami, a big black wave, full of bones and skulls and making its way over to us, knowing we're all going to die.

So I started gardening. My sister-in-law was sending me seeds from California because we were all sold out of seeds, we were all sold out of potting soil, we were sold out of everything. We are an island. It was frightening. I was just holding on for dear life to my poodle.

Doing the PPE work connected me to other people in the community, and that was scary too. Doctors and nurses were creating their own emergency phone trees so they knew who to call when the first wave of doctors and nurses got sick. They were figuring out how to liaise with different hospitals in the state of Hawaii, and it was all grassroots. It was so grassroots that it was terrifying. It was so crazy, what was going on.

This whole pandemic has showed me personally, and I'm sure millions of other people, that we can do hard things, and we can get through this. Maybe next time if something really terrible happens, we'll at least know this about ourselves.

Hawaii
June 2021

Some mask opponents asked me if I felt stupid for getting COVID.

Jan-Michele

Councilwoman and Publisher

As a community newspaper, people call our staff for everything. We're supposed to know everybody and everything. People were calling, saying, "I heard that a mixture of bleach helps and how much do you put in." There was a rumor, could be they heard this from somebody in Washington, that drinking bleach helps prevent COVID. We told them *zero* percent bleach—you cannot drink bleach, that will kill you. You can wash surfaces with bleach, but do not ingest it.

People were just so desperate, and they were inundated with information and misinformation. Do this, don't do that, go here, don't go there, be outside, open your window, stay inside, stay home, eat this food, don't eat that food, touch this, don't touch that. There was too much information, and much of it was wrong, which is why several of us joined together to do town hall meetings every Saturday.

We did a lot of talking about masks, and I was one of the cosponsors and pushers of the city council's mask ordinance. I firmly believe it's important to wear masks to help other people even if you don't think it's going to help you. I became a living example of this when I got COVID in August. The day before I started to feel sick, I had been working with two new interns in my office and they were there with me all day, all of us wearing masks. I asked them to get tested, and my husband and I went for testing also. My husband's and both interns' results were negative, thank goodness. Unfortunately, my COVID-19 test was positive.

I went on Twitter and told my story. I put it out there because I don't want it to be a stigma. I want people to know they shouldn't feel ashamed about getting COVID. My tweet had more than 31,000 impressions—COVID is a hot topic. Being one of the mask ordinance proponents on City Council, some mask opponents asked me if I felt stupid for getting COVID. I said "No, because my interns were with me and they didn't get it." This is a good example that wearing a mask helps to keep others safe.

Ohio
September 2020

We couldn't read the room. It was just a four-year-old in a mask. All we could see were his eyes.

Liz

Clown

I miss people and laughter, particularly kid laughter. When you have a room of 500 five-year-olds, it's like conducting an orchestra of laughter, and there's nothing greater than that.

When the hospital called and asked if I would do my clown doctoring virtually, I said yes. I have no training in the virtual world, and nobody I asked knew how to do it.

Leo and I put on our clown doctor coats and our noses, collected our props, set up a backdrop in my kitchen, and the hospital brought the laptop into a room with a kid. Suddenly we're on, and there's this kid. Usually you read the room, get a sense of how sick the kid is, how they are feeling, whether their parents are there. We couldn't read the room. It was just a four-year-old in a mask. All we could see were his eyes.

We were with that kid for about thirty minutes, but it felt like a twelve-hour day. It was the hardest performance I've ever had in my life. After the first twenty minutes we stopped. I could barely speak. All my experience, thirty years of performing, we tried everything. And then we realized, like with a cartoon, the simplest thing. The kid said "Boo" and Leo ran off the screen. The kid said "Boo" again and Leo ran off the screen again. The kid cracked up. We did that for ten minutes. But it took us forever to find that moment.

Once we got that, I thought, *Oh, I can do this! It's comedy, all it is is comedy, and the simpler and the stupider and the more clear it is, like old slapstick, the better.* So then I got a rubber chicken and I hit the screen with the chicken and Leo went like this with the chicken and fell down. And that's all we needed.

Connecticut
August 2020

44

*I've been running with Old Glory since
March 13, all over the state of Arkansas.*

Nate

Arkansas Running Man

My mission started back on March 11 when
COVID-19 hit Arkansas. That's when my whole journey started. It was
placed in my heart when our town had a town hall meeting about
COVID-19. I was trying to think of what I can do to help this community. I wanted my community to stay strong and stay uplifted, and God
placed it in my spirit to pick up Old Glory and run.

I served in the U.S. Army infantry from 1987 through 1995. Combat
vet. Served in Korea; Germany; Fort Hood in Texas; Fort Carson, Colorado; Fort Benning, Georgia. Love my military. Very proudly served,
and I still serve even when I'm out because once a vet always a vet, once
a soldier always a soldier. Old Glory is very close to me.

I've been running with Old Glory since March 13, all over the state
of Arkansas. Northeast, southwest central, the largest town, the smallest towns. I've been doing it, and I'm continuing to do it, to keep everyone uplifted and inspired. I've calculated over 882 miles and, thus
far, six pairs of tennis shoes.

All the towns love what I'm doing. In this trying time that we are in
right now, people like to see something positive. Remind them this is
our country, we're better than this, we're going to make it through this.
That's why I care. I am so proud and I just love my country.

I'm born and raised in Arkansas, about thirty minutes south of
here. My home, population eighty-nine people. So very small, but
we have the biggest hearts. Smallest towns have some of the biggest
hearts. They are so warm, and they give so much and look out for
one another. I love people. I love my country, and definitely love me
some Old Glory. That red, white, and blue says a lot. We really should

be loving our country right now because the sacrifice, the ultimate sacrifice, has already been paid. Too much blood has been shed. So that's why we got to stand strong with the country now during these trying times.

I really care about people, and I want people to get back to loving one another. That's all we got to do; everything else will take care of itself. Get back to the basic humanity of loving one another from the heart. Everything else—title, position, politics, race, religion, all that—it will take care of itself. Get back to the basic humanity of treating people the way you want to be treated. We learned that as children, very small children. You learn how to be good, how to be kind, how to be polite. Our parents and grandparents, they taught us that as children. We got to get back to it. I'm a human being, you're a human being. You look right at the heart of a person, and things take care of itself. It'll take care of itself. Always have, always will.

Arkansas
October 2020

It didn't seem fair that we got to keep our doors open while other people had to close their doors.

Aaron

Restaurant Relief Organizer

I was always taught to love your neighbor and that when a crisis strikes, everybody should get together, all hands on deck. The ones who are able to help should help and the ones who need help should receive help. Because at some point, the roles are going to reverse. You survive things together.

In February, when we first started hearing about COVID, nobody knew what it was about, nobody knew what was going on. Then it started becoming more localized, and we started getting cases in Oklahoma, and everybody was trying to figure out what in the world's going on here, is the world fixing to come to an end. There were people that were just kind of panicky, and people didn't want to leave their houses. Then businesses were closing down, businesses were shutting their doors. A lot of the smaller restaurants weren't equipped for the drive-through or the curbside pickup or anything like that. They didn't know what to do. They were just thrust into this problem.

Our company, Covington Aircraft, was declared essential, so we were able to keep our doors open. It didn't seem fair to us that we got to keep our doors open, keep people employed, while other people had to close their doors in times of need, in times of struggle.

We started looking at what we could do to keep our employees safe, so that when they came on-site to work, they stayed here for the day and weren't running around to different places in town to get lunch and maybe pick up the virus. We also started looking at ways we could help our community of Okmulgee to try to salvage our friends' businesses.

I called my friend Heather, who runs Okmulgee Main Street, and asked what our company could do to help some of the local restaurants.

We started brainstorming ideas and came up with the idea of having a group of restaurants cater the meals for our employees every day.

Then I called my friends who run other companies, told them what Covington was doing, and suggested they do the same with some of the other restaurants. If we could salvage those restaurants and get together as a community, then maybe everybody would still have a business to come back to when we get to the other side of this thing. I was calling banks, I was calling car dealerships and different companies like that. They all said they would figure out what they could do.

It kind of rallied the whole community, to say, "Hey, we can take care of ourselves. We know all this other stuff is going on in the world, but we're going to survive this because we're all looking out for each other."

Oklahoma
October 2020

....

Every time a relief check comes out, or COVID *check or whatever you want to call it, it just ramps it up again.*

Tim

Liquor Store Manager

When the first stimulus checks came out and the bars were closed, everybody came to us. It was kind of like, "Well, can't go to a bar. Let's get our own bottle and sit at the house." The first three weeks, we were doing triple the sales of what we normally do. Our Fridays and Saturdays were like Christmas Eve and New Year's Eve. Just unbelievable numbers. We had to start closing early just to get some rest. It was a dead run from the time we opened till the time we closed. We started closing at eight o'clock just for employees to get some rest.

The state ABC board, supply department, and dispatch were all immediately overwhelmed, too. So the state put limits on how much they would ship out each day, hoping they could keep up with that. Now, just about a year later, we're down probably 50 percent of where it first started with triple sales, but it is still just unbelievable. Our numbers are huge, and the state still can't keep up. The state is currently two weeks behind on shipping. Before COVID, they would ship next day.

We're back to normal hours now, but it's still a whooping. And who knows when it's going to end. Every time a relief check comes out, or COVID check or whatever you want to call it, it just ramps it up again. Extra money is not going to food. I think a lot of it's going to party.

Mississippi
March 2021

49

It is important that whatever blessings a community has be shared with our fellow citizens.

Azhar

Relief Organization Director

I was distributing food boxes one day when a lady who had recently lost her husband drove through the pickup line. In the car with her were her children. The food boxes we distributed could sustain a family for a good two to three weeks. The woman said to me, "I am going through one of the most difficult times of my life. I have three children and I don't have anything to feed them. Can I please get an extra box?" We gave her two extra boxes. Not only would one box sustain and help her for fifteen days, but these three boxes would help her for maybe a month or month and a half, and during that time she could focus on other things rather than worrying about how to feed her children. Like so many of the people who came to get the food, her situation was heartbreaking.

Also in the pickup line were people who had been leading pretty comfortable lives. One man drove up in a nice car and I was wondering, "He's in such an expensive car, why is he here to pick up boxes of food?" Then the man himself looked at me and said, "You may be thinking that I have plenty by looking at my car. But I have not paid the installments, I'm back on my payments, and I lost my job. This food box will definitely help me and my family."

Sometimes there were tears in people's eyes, and other times people were at a complete loss for words. We were particularly concerned about the elderly who couldn't get to the distribution centers, so our volunteers went to their homes to see what they needed. Some were in desperate need of medicine, but they were too scared to leave their homes to go pick it up. The volunteers did that for them. And the joy we saw on their faces was priceless.

There were also times when we distributed cash cards for fifty or a hundred dollars so people could buy essential items or items of personal need that they may not be comfortable asking a stranger for at a public food distribution site. We could see the sparkle that was in their eyes when they were receiving the cards.

Our motto at Islamic Relief USA is to offer aid and assistance in a dignified manner. Because anybody can be in that situation. We live in a country where sometimes people live from paycheck to paycheck, so there are challenging times, and anybody can be in this kind of situation.

It is important that whatever blessings a community has be shared with our fellow citizens. We have to thank God for every blessing he has bestowed upon us, and also at the same time think about our fellow human beings, our fellow citizens, and respond to them when they are in need of help and assistance.

Our holy scriptures remind us that after every hardship, there is a relief. I am optimistic that the good days are ahead of us. We were very blessed to be able to play a role in the lives of those individuals who were going through some very difficult times. Once they get back to normalcy, get back to their jobs, they will remember and do their best to assist others.

Texas
June 2021

Most of these guys have been in prison for long
enough that they don't know how to use tablets,
surf the internet, set up email accounts.

Stewart

Prisoner Support Volunteer

I volunteer at San Quentin State Prison, and since March we have not been able to go back in. As you know, there's a massive number of people being released because of COVID-19.

When they are released, there are many fear factors, of which COVID is only one. "How do I find housing? How do I eat? How do I take care of myself? How do I find work? Who's hiring? Will my record keep me from getting a job?" They give them a couple days to live in a motel or something, and then they have to support themselves.

If they stay in contact with the probation department for the first two weeks, doing everything they're supposed to do, they are given a computer tablet so they can do required virtual visits with probation officers, search for jobs, and do online support programs. The problem is that most of these guys have been in prison for long enough that they don't know how to use tablets, surf the internet, set up email accounts. For us, the internet is simple. But not for them. Many of them don't even know how to operate a cell phone. Now they are being given these tablets and told to get on the internet.

Before COVID, organizations like mine would meet with these men in person and get a sense of the kind of support and counseling they needed. The men were actively coming to the classes and getting treatment before COVID. But they don't want to do Zoom. We have a lot of online program materials, but they don't want to do online, FaceTime, or anything like that. They don't understand it's the same thing because they haven't lived on the outside for so long. We tell them that it's just like you being in front of me. We have to get them past this fear, teach them and tell them it's okay. Just click the link and then the person who is there to help you is right in front of you.

California
September 2020

For the first time, it was safer to be outside rather than inside.

Anne

Homeless Shelter Director

The way homeless sheltering has always worked is you pack as many people inside a building as you can because it is safer to be inside rather than outside.

COVID changed all of that because, for the first time, it was safer to be outside rather than inside. Because we are in Alabama, with its warmer climate, it was okay to say, "We're at capacity, you can sleep around the building or go to the parks." When it started getting cold again, we had to ask ourselves, "Do you fill the building to capacity and potentially have a COVID outbreak, or do you let people risk it sleeping outside?" Every day, it felt like a little bit of a Sophie's choice.

When we moved into our new building in March, we were at capacity with seventy people. By mid-March, we were probably up to eighty-five. Then everything started shutting down, and the health department told us to reduce our numbers drastically. After about four weeks, we were at fifty.

Our goal was to keep everyone on-site all throughout the day. So obviously, being in a homeless shelter with people in active addiction, all of a sudden our folks couldn't get to their doctors, they couldn't get medication. Telling them they could not leave the facility was an absolute nightmare. It really hit a boiling point around May when we started having some turnover. It was like having a live grenade every time you let someone in off the street.

For the first time in our history, we had an episode of violence. It was two people that had untreated mental health issues. One of them, about twenty years old, had been dismissed for using drugs on the property. When he came back a few days later, we let him in because everywhere else was closed down. One of the gentlemen ended up losing his life.

That was really the boiling point for our organization. We like to say we're a big happy family, and everyone had gotten kind of relaxed because we spent so much time here with the same people. I think we forgot how many barriers these guys are facing and the lack of adequate mental health care. People were cooped up and away from their families with no outlet.

What happened changed the dynamic of the agency in a very real sense because for the first time we were screening who was coming in. That felt awful because the homeless folks that have mental health issues are the ones that need help the very most. On top of that, everyone who had been at the shelter when it happened was suffering from trauma. The staff was nervous because no one saw this coming. And we were still dealing with COVID.

We're up to seventy again, which isn't where we need to be. We do our best with social distancing, but when you're dealing with a population in which a lot of people have mental health disorders like schizophrenia, having people's mouths covered isn't great.

As of a month ago, we had not had one client come up positive for COVID. We don't require tests to come in and stay at the shelter. When someone comes in and they haven't had a test, we put them in quarantine. They are not allowed to leave until we find a place to get them tested. And then they can go out with the rest of the folks. It has worked really well.

But then a month ago, we had two guys that came in and they had COVID. One guy caught it at work, but his room in the shelter was in quarantine. The other guy had just gotten out of prison and he went to stay with his mom. That situation wasn't working out well and he really wanted to come to the shelter. We asked him the standard list of questions. He said "No, no, no, no." Three days later, he mentioned in passing that he hadn't been able to smell or taste anything. And his mom had COVID, which he knew coming into the shelter, but he wanted to get out of her house. Luckily, he was in quarantine, and we were able to get him a hotel. So we didn't have an outbreak.

Alabama
January 2021

I wonder how many people passed because we just gave up.

Anonymous

Doctor

I take every patient as if they're my own flesh and blood and I want to make sure that they do their best. If it's time for them to go, we understand that and we have that long discussion. But not knowing what this novel coronavirus did to people and not knowing the long-term effects, you have to fight for the individual rather than follow protocols that do not make sense to you from a clinical standpoint.

The hospital insisted that we paralyze one of my patients while he was on a ventilator to prevent him from extubating himself. I'm like, "What difference does it make? We can reintubate him if that happens." Anytime you paralyze anyone for a prolonged length of time, you get muscle atrophy, and it's very difficult to have those people recover.

Finally, after a significant amount of ranting and raving, I was able to stop that. The consensus I had was that I probably should have let him die. Of course, those words are typically not in my vocabulary.

I'm very happy that he made it through, and he's welcome at my house anytime. I hug his wife at the grocery store every time I see her, and him as well.

You know, I wonder how many people passed because we just gave up. For me, it's been a very difficult pill to swallow.

I still treat patients my same way and have been very successful in a lot of ways. Some are unsuccessful. It's a bad disease, I know that. It's something that we will have to come to grips with in the future, because I don't see this pandemic taking another hundred years before it occurs again.

Louisiana
January 2021

The kids are watching us. I think they're proud of us, that we got out there and that we decided we've got to save our town.

Brenda

Downtown Leader

We've been doing cash mobs here in Raton since 2010. When COVID hit and our downtown stores closed, we knew that a cash mob, a really big, sustained one, was needed more than ever. It's always been an in-person event, though, so we had to figure out how to do it online.

We decided to do it as a two-hour Facebook Live show, twice a week in different stores. A few of us went into the store and showed off the products, almost like a QVC show. We had a great, great following. Each night, we had an average of 100 people watching. We did this for twelve weeks, and the result was terrific. Some of our businesses made $3,500 in two hours. And for a small business, that's a lot of money. Some of the businesses also have gained new customers after being featured, so that's really exciting.

In total, the Facebook Live Raton Cash Mob helped thirty-one different businesses in our community and generated more than $40,000 in sales revenues. This meant the businesses were able to pay their utilities and their rents and, you know, stay open even though they were closed to everything except curbside online sales. Another benefit was that the businesses learned how to use online payment platforms; a lot of the stores are using them now.

Everybody in town got involved, even some of the kids who had grown up and moved out of town. One of the hosts, Melissa, has a son in the navy who was watching from Florida. He told his mom there was an easier way to track the sales. So these kids, they came up with Google Sheets, Google Forms, as the method. They would be at home watching the live Facebook feed and tracking who bought what. By the end of the night, we could hand it to the business owner and say, "This is what sold, this is who bought it. Now you can invoice them through your Square or PayPal or however you're going to do it and set up delivery or pickup options with them."

It occurred to me during one of the shows that the kids are watching us. I think they're proud of us, that we got out there and that we decided we've got to save our town. They have a love for their hometown, just like we do, and they really wanted to help us out.

You see this rock that says "YOU" on it? It's my "You Rock" award for helping out. Best award ever.

New Mexico
October 2020

*If the choice is to close or go down with a fight,
I'm fighting, because I've worked too hard for too
long.*

Jeannie

Vintage Clothing Store Owner

Closing was bittersweet because we had the best day, sales-wise, that Saturday before we closed. I think it was the first weekend in March, and boom, the world changed the next week. Still very naively, I thought, *Well, I'll close for one month and I'll get some stuff done.*

When I could open again, I started with outdoor sales. My shop has a large parking lot out back and porches everywhere, wrapping around the house. The first time I did an outdoor sale, I didn't know what the numbers were going to look like. Because everyone is in the same boat as far as, "Maybe we shouldn't spend any money." If you're lucky and have two people with two jobs, that's great, but a lot of people aren't that lucky—they either lost their job or had to stay at home to take care of their kids when the schools went online. I don't take anything for granted.

For that first outdoor sale, it was about getting through my fear and my anxiety. This either was going to work or not. I sell vintage clothes, so I had no idea if people would buy clothes off a rack outside. I said to my friend who was helping me, "You know what, we may be sitting here looking at each other, and we're good. There may be tears and there may be prosecco involved, but we're going to get through it."

I think a maximum of twenty people or something was allowed at a gathering at that time, so I got on my phone and texted my core group of customers. Eighteen came out—a small group, but it's what I needed because I was terrified with what to do about COVID and customers anyway.

You can't help but think you're going to get sick every time you come into contact with someone, and I can't do my job without coming into contact with someone. So getting through that first outdoor sale was key. The next day, the next two days, we did really well, but I just needed to get my feet wet. I needed to get over my anxiety and to know that I could do this.

I hate to say it, but there's not one thing that you have to have that's in this store. I believe in it and I love everything that I have in here, but you can't eat it. You can survive without it. And you may possibly be putting yourself at risk if you're around other people. Every single one of those things crosses my mind still every day when I open. So I'm very, very grateful for anyone that comes to my door, and whether they buy anything or not, they're trying just as hard as I am.

If the choice is to close or go down with a fight, I'm fighting, because I've worked too hard for too long—fifteen years—and built something I really care about. I'm not going to have it go down like this.

North Carolina
November 2020

Everybody felt they should be first.

Jackie

Salon Owner

In the beginning of the spring, there was a lot of anxiety about continuing to stay open as the number of COVID cases rose. There was so much unknown about the virus and how contagious it was and how it was spread. At that point in time, we thought if we went and touched an apple in the grocery store that somebody else had touched, we were going to get COVID.

I stayed open until the governor shut us down. And for about two weeks leading up to closing on March 25, I was already wearing a mask, making clients wash their hands, not double-booking. I worked ten days in a row in order to get everybody in. The writing was on the wall.

And honestly, truth be told, there was a little bit of excitement about having some indeterminate amount of time to myself. For the last eleven years, the longest time I had been off of work was one week. One week. And so after about three or four weeks, I was kind of enjoying it.

When I reopened, I really struggled with how to rebook clients. I have almost 300 clients and everybody felt they should be first, and for good reason. The people who were canceled right after we closed thought they should be first; the people who had standing appointments a week before we reopened thought they should be first. So I decided to raffle off my appointments and give the money to PORCH, which collects food for those in need. I expected to raise maybe $1,000. I think 173 clients participated. The more tickets they bought, the higher up they got on my list. I raised $4,500.

North Carolina
August 2020

61

If we chose RV living, we would lose less money
than if I got a temporary job somewhere and
stayed in the big house.

Chris and Molly

Airline Pilot and Wife

CHRIS: In April, airline passenger loads
dropped to 5 percent of what they were the year prior. You can't run
any business that way, so the airlines started canceling flights and
parking planes. I am on the junior side of the seniority list, so my wife
and I knew we had to set ourselves up financially to ride out what was
looking to be a long furlough.

MOLLY: We had a big house in Texas, 3,900 square feet with a
pool in the backyard and a huge three-car garage. That garage could
fit everything, even the jet ski we won on *Let's Make a Deal*, but that's
another story.

CHRIS: We prepared for the worst and started kicking around
some ideas. One option was to stay in the house we were in while I
got a temporary job somewhere, like Lowe's or Home Depot. Pilots
don't have appreciable skills that can easily translate into another
field, so an entry-level job was most likely. Another option was that
we could sell the house and buy a smaller house to reduce the mort-
gage payment a bit. The third option was to downsize even further,
into an RV.

And I'm like, all right, well, we're going to lose a lot of cash one way
or another. In late April and early May, we were running the numbers,
and it was clear that if we chose RV living, we would lose less money
than if I got a temporary job somewhere and stayed in the big house.
And that was RV living with no job, like no income at all.

I was thinking, *I will have no other time in my life where I will be home
with my kids for more than a week or two at a time.* With the airline, I'm

usually gone half the month. And looking at the ages of our kids—three, five, and seven—that was really important to me.

MOLLY: We were a little familiar with living in an RV because we'd rented an RV in February and had absolutely loved it. We spent ten days visiting national and state parks in Nevada, Utah, and Arizona. It was a lot of fun. We'd actually spent a few years thinking and dreaming about that trip before we did it. We had done our research and felt that RVing could be something we'd really enjoy. We take a lot of trips as an airline family and have a great time trying out new adventures, so the RV life seemed like a good fit. And that trip was just so much fun that it put something in our minds and our hearts like, *We could live in an RV.*

When May rolled around, we hadn't made a decision yet, but we knew we were tired of being cooped up in our house. We had to leave. So we went to visit some of our friends in Florida. When we mentioned the whole RV thing, they were like, "Y'all are crazy. That sounds fun for a hot sec, but you're not going to like it long-term. You're going to get sick of being in such a small place with your kids and all that." And we're like, "No, no, no."

Near the end of May, we went to visit some friends of ours from Instagram. We hadn't met them in person yet, but they RV full-time and we just wanted to go and ask them questions, hang out, see their RV. We asked them a bajillion questions about RV life, and they gave us a lot of good advice. The best advice they gave us was just do it, just to go for it. And, you know, the worst thing that can happen is that it doesn't work out and you just go back to your old life.

CHRIS: A week later, on June 1, we bought a forty-three-foot fifth-wheel toy hauler. On June 3, we listed our house. Actually, the house sold the day before it was technically listed, for asking price, even though it was at the high end of what all the realtors were saying. Now I wish I had gone higher, of course, but it's also nice to have gotten rid of it and be done with it.

It's now May 2021 and we've traveled about 10,000 miles all over the United States. I'm present here with my family, taking adventures. We don't regret selling the house and moving into a fifth wheel. You know, traveling around and doing what we're doing, we don't regret it at all, and we have no future date set for when we're going to stop or go part-time with it or anything like that.

We're about to enter into a different season, with going back to work. In March, they announced they were bringing back all the pilots as soon as October. In June, I will be going back to training.

MOLLY: We'll be traveling in our RV, staying at campgrounds. When Chris has a flight, I'll drop him off in our truck, he'll go and do his trip, and then I'll go pick him back up. When his trip is done, we can go explore.

Living in the RV has created this life of adventure, and we love it. It's like the thing where life gives you lemons. We got lemons and then we turned them into something cool and crazy and awesome.

Texas
April 2021

I'm a pretty tough cookie. Figuring out how to survive isn't hard for me.

Kay

Hair Salon Owner

2020 was a terrible year. I had a salon inside a retirement community. I was shut down before anybody in town. I was shut down until July, well after everything opened back up. So, no work, no pay. And it took over twelve weeks to get unemployment approved.

Then, after I was allowed to open back up, the retirement community closed me down every time someone may have been exposed. It happened on a weekly basis, over and over. They had me shut down more than I was open, but I still had to pay them the full month's rent. It cost me a fortune.

I'm a pretty tough cookie, though. I lived on the streets when I was twelve years old, I raised three boys on my own, and I boxed for five years. So figuring out how to survive isn't hard for me, it's just a matter of doing it without repercussions. I wound up making my kitchen a salon for about four months and going to people's houses to cut hair. I had to.

I'm pretty sure my neighbors thought I was a hooker with the amount of men coming in and out of my house. They left the house looking a whole lot better than when they came in.

Montana
June 2021

Comedy clubs are ripe for the spread of coronavirus.

Jeremy

Stand-Up Comedian

I did a show in New York the night before they shut down everything. Everything was still open, so we decided to take the trip and just make sure we washed our hands a lot and social-distanced. We didn't bring masks. At the time, people didn't really know how it was spreading. It was when people were washing their groceries and wiping down their mail. I did a show on our first day there. On the second day, we went to a museum. While we were there, they announced over the loudspeakers that they would be closing early. The governor was shutting down all public buildings.

It was just starting to dawn on people: this was serious. I remember we ate in a restaurant. We went and had a drink at a bar, and we're like, "Oh, there's one that's still open, let's get in there before they shut it down." And in retrospect, that was crazy. If we had had a black light and been able to see all the germs, we probably would have gone home, but we didn't know. No one knew. New York City was a cesspool of COVID, and we had no idea when we were there that it was as widespread as it was.

I thought things would go back to normal. Turns out, it was much worse than we realized. At the end of March, there was a big comedy festival I was supposed to do in North Carolina. They ended up canceling that. And then it was just like dominoes, all these festivals I was planning to do, shows I was supposed to do, all started to fall, one after the other.

When some clubs reopened, I had to make a decision, as we all did in the community. What were we comfortable with doing as comedians? In what venues, what situations, were we willing to perform?

Since I didn't have to continue doing comedy to survive because I had a day job, I decided not to perform inside, both for my personal safety and because I also don't want to encourage people to gather. My grandmother died of COVID earlier this year. That's always on my mind.

I think comedy clubs in particular are ripe for the spread of coronavirus because laughter, singing, loud talking, any of that just sends the virus, and you get that from both directions. Comedians are loud and they're spewing, and audience members are loud and they're spewing. And a lot of comedy clubs are very densely packed places—not great circulation, low ceilings.

I did a handful of shows on Zoom and Facebook Live and Instagram, and it was just awful. It was just the worst experience. Just throwing your jokes into the void. People aren't used to being on Zoom and listening to comedy, so if you turn everybody's mics on, all of a sudden, you're hearing what everybody's doing in their bedrooms and living rooms across the country while you're telling jokes. People making margaritas in the background, dogs barking, and babies crying, and people doing what they do in beds. I'm glad that I did the few that I did, but I did learn pretty quickly, like, this was soul crushing. I decided not to do any more online shows.

When the weather got warmer and people could be served drinks outside, I resumed our monthly comedy show, *The Sunday Show*, at Yonder, a bar in Hillsborough. That first night back was great, with a terrific crowd. It was really a lot of fun. And right now, I can get any comic in North Carolina to come perform because they're all so desperate for stage time. "Yeah, I'll drive three hours to some town I've never heard of for twenty bucks as long as there's a chance for me to tell my jokes for ten minutes."

The next month, I got sick a couple days before the show. I got tested, but the test had a seventy-two-hour turnaround. So I decided I wouldn't participate in my own show. It was right around that time that things started spiking again in North Carolina, and I decided at that point that I no longer felt comfortable hosting the show, even though it's outside. It felt like too much of a risk for me, and I didn't want to put other people at risk.

I don't know what stand-up is going to be like when this is over. So many comedy clubs went out of business. I think it's going to be a while before people are comfortable packing together in tiny rooms and listening to people tell jokes.

I also don't know if people are going to want to hear COVID humor when this is all over. Are we going to want to talk about it, to laugh about it? We won't know until we start getting up in front of audiences again and trying corona jokes.

North Carolina
December 2020

I've always wanted to start a clothing line, and 2020 was the perfect time.

Ine'a

College Student and Entrepreneur

I wanted to do something during the pandemic. I'm twenty-one years old and I couldn't really go anywhere. I'm the type of person who loves to be on Instagram, taking a lot of pictures, going on trips and doing extravagant things, and we couldn't really do that in the pandemic. I wanted to do something that was impactful and be able to say that I did that when I was twenty-one. So I launched an e-commerce retailing business called The Repertoire. It's my "2020 vision."

When I was younger, I used to want to be a fashion designer. I've always wanted to start a clothing line, and 2020 was the perfect time for me to sit down and take the time to start it, even though I was already busy. I had three online classes; I was working at a juice bar within a health food store, which was considered an essential store during the pandemic; and I was doing my online internship. But I knew that I needed to start my business and do something for me.

My first collection is called the Butterfly Collection. In college we're so young, there's a lot of growth going on, and it's a beautiful thing. You have your own wings. I've been blessed with so much, and I see myself blossom more and more into my own butterfly. There's so much more growth that will happen for myself and my business, and I find that truly beautiful.

I wanted to do a big launch party and invite friends and family so people could come and see my products, but that couldn't happen because of the pandemic. I started off small, doubting myself and thinking that even if no one buys anything, it's okay as long as I get to wear it, and family members can purchase from me if need be. I'm happy to say that my business is doing a lot better than I even thought it would. In a few weeks, I'll be doing a pop-up shop in my friend's boutique inside our university's student center. My 2021 goal is to market to more people than just those around me and expand The Repertoire.

The Repertoire's motto is "Embrace the uncomfortable and walk with purpose." That's what I'm doing.

Missouri
September 2020

We can't even take off to go fishing because we have to make cornhole boards.

Jared and Kerry

Founders, Beens' Workshop

JARED: My brother, Kerry, and I are both pipeliners by trade. I was laid off in January and Kerry was laid off in November when oil prices had dropped. Companies had quit building, quit drilling, quit laying pipe. Prices had just started picking up when COVID kind of took over and prices plummeted again. What happened next was the start of Beens' Workshop. Somebody hit me up on Facebook and asked if we could build them a set of cornhole boards. Kerry has a shop in his backyard and has built furniture in there. We built the first cornhole set, not really having a clue on how to do it. From there, it just kind of took off overnight. We made a Facebook page and it's been nonstop ever since. Even when we tried to slow it down, it didn't slow. We tried. We even raised the price and people still kept pouring in. As time went on, we were improving on our skills. That news started to spread more and more.

KERRY: We've turned out quality work, so we are kept busy with return customers and new customers through word of mouth and customer referrals, even from other states. We've been shipping these heavy boards to other states, and people have been coming here from other states as well to pick them up. We stay busy. It's just Jared and me. We need to figure out the next step in this endeavor.

JARED: It's true, because we can't even take off to go fishing because we have to make cornhole boards. The whole purpose was just to try to make a little extra money. It was just a hobby for us. We wanted to have a hobby that made us a little money, allowed us to fish and hunt and do the things we wanted to do, like spend time with our families.

KERRY: Now it's turned into a business. And I hate to say this, but

71

COVID was the perfect storm for us. People were told to stay home. Cornhole gave them something to do, and it's a game everybody can play.

JARED: When there were no professional sports on television, ESPN was showing cornhole all the time. Since it's an outside game, people can social-distance. And organizations have been hosting cornhole tournaments as fundraisers.

KERRY: It was perfect for us. I am sorry to say that because so many people lost jobs and things, but at the same time COVID is the reason I didn't go back to work. COVID shut down some of the big jobs I was supposed to go on. It kind of worked out both ways; it was a good thing and it was a bad thing. For a lot of people, it has been a bad thing, but for us, as a small business getting started, it was perfect.

Oklahoma
October 2020

My life has just turned into work.

Liz

Remote Worker

My home has been my office for almost two years, so the working-from-home part is not that different, but it's making me realize how much I valued everything else in my life. Before all of this, I had a full life outside of work, between going to my exercise classes, visiting my mom, going out with friends, traveling, or doing stuff around the city. So it's been really hard to have to suddenly give everything up, even though I know it's for the greater good.

And I found that my life has just turned into work, that I work all the time. I get up, make coffee, I get dressed, and I come and sit down and work until seven o'clock. The result is that my business is growing. I enjoy my work, so it's an easy habit to fall into. But, conversely, I've gained a ton of weight, and all I do is work. That's it. At the beginning, I tried to keep the same routine I had before, exercising at home, seeing friends and family for virtual visits. But it quickly started to feel pointless. I can tell that I am not really okay. My therapist is, well, worried about me. I know it's not good to see work as my only purpose, so I'm conscious of that, but at the same time it's like, what else is there?

Washington, D.C.
August 2020

People need expression and an outlet for grief or stress or unexpected challenges of life.

Sementha

Art Museum Director

What we've come to understand, probably more than ever before, is how your life cannot be just an individual life revolving around yourself and your job. While jobs are certainly what sustains us for livability, expenses, and obligations that we have, there are so many different elements to life—your social life, your creative life, your emotional life. The absence of some of these elements is what we've seen people dealing with, but sometimes in really bad ways.

People need expression and an outlet for grief or stress or unexpected challenges of life. We in the arts should be the healers, the artistic doctors that come out and say, "This is a way that you can deal with your anxieties and your stress. We know it doesn't put food on the table, but it helps you think clearly, and it helps you process life and deal with what you're going through."

We moved our classes outside so we could reach as many people as needed us, including people who maybe didn't know they needed the arts. Whether it is our outdoor music performances or some of our classes, like ukulele, pottery, writing, or photography, there is something for everyone, a way to help capture emotion or whatever you're going through and allow you a chance to breathe and deal with it and grow from it.

Georgia
December 2020

Maria

Women's Wellness Advocate

I am someone who has depression. In January of 2020, I was clawing my way out, using all kinds of modalities I have learned to help me. Then COVID hit. I, like so many people I know, became very fearful about what might happen.

But as time wore on, my life necessarily slowed down so much that I gave myself permission not to think about the future. I talk about future-tripping as one of my character defects. I used to worry incessantly about the future, but coronavirus and the pandemic and the restrictions on travel and on things we can do actually became a benefit to me, because there was no more fear of missing out.

The pandemic caused me to not make any plans for the future, because there weren't that many things that were available to do. And there was so much uncertainty that planning was almost futile. I was forced to be more present. And I was forced to evaluate what I liked about my life and what was working in my life and to focus on things for which I am grateful.

And I was forced to slow down every aspect of my life and to just be rather than to keep doing. Sometimes I joke that I'm a "human doing" instead of a human being. The pandemic required me to breathe more consciously and relax more. There was nothing to do at night. Nobody was having parties or outings or meetings, except online. I had a lot more time. I wasn't commuting anymore. I could work from home. And with the extra time, my blood pressure went down because I was simply doing less—and getting by with less, and having less to organize. I'm a perpetual organizer. And traveler. Traveling is one of my favorite things to do. But there was nowhere to go.

So everything seemed to slow for me, in a good way. And I gave myself permission to slow down, which is contrary to my normal disposition. I'm always on the go. People used to think there was something wrong with me because I cannot sit and watch a television show without doing something else, because TV seems like a waste of time. And I don't know why I was so obsessed with time in that way. Wasting time was almost a sin for me. But I don't worry about that anymore.

I have adjusted to a new way of being and have realigned what my version of success is, what my vision of a content and fulfilling life is for me, and I'm in a much better place. I focused on gratitude. I've inserted an easy exercise regimen into my life. I've learned my own brand of minimalism, partially out of necessity, because of the virus and things that are closed and not wanting to expose myself to unnecessary germs. But it has had a ripple effect in many areas of my life that I would not have anticipated. And that resulted in the calmer Maria you see today.

So, as odd as it is to say, the pandemic helped me reset my life. And today, I'm actually in a much better place than I was on January 1, 2020. And I attribute a lot of that to the pandemic's forced reset and slowdown of my life.

Maryland
November 2020

*No one has written what the protocol is when
a domestic violence event is happening during
Zoom.*

Iris

Women's Recovery Center Counselor

The changes necessitated by COVID had a pro-
found effect on the women we see through the recovery center's outpatient program. Most of these women have been referred to us by
the Department of Child and Family Services, and they are not per-
mitted to have their children back until they go through the program
successfully.

One of the things that keeps these women actively working the
program week after week is knowing they will earn visits with their
children. Moms usually get at least two visits a week for four hours
minimum of program participation. And then, if it's going well, they
start to be able to have overnights. We know how important bonding
is for the mom and the baby, so the aim is to preserve the family unit.
If there's any way to do it, then that's what you want to do.

But in-person visits were not possible for many months at the beginning of the pandemic. If the child was in a kinship home with a
relative, DCFS was more flexible. If the child was in a foster home, the
wait for a visit was about six months. It was a long, long, long time, and
in the meantime it was Zoom visits. I mean, it was understandable.
There were no vaccines at that point, kids often don't display symptoms, and the foster families were taking a risk of taking in a child.
Also, foster families would need to leave the house to bring the child to
the birth mom because policies prevent the birth mom from knowing
where the child is living.

It was a complete unraveling of so many things. In addition, DCFS was fairly remote for a period of time, so the case managers weren't even available. Zoom helped, but it also created new challenges.

We've always done our group and individual counseling in person. When we moved it to Zoom, it moved the sessions into whatever environment the participants were in at the time the session was happening. Women were turning cameras off, and we would have no sense of whether they're even there. There also were domestic violence events a few times while the group sessions were happening. These women are living in poverty, maybe in a one-bedroom apartment, and their partner is in the house and an argument starts. The counselor would create a breakout group and we'd try to assess the situation for safety, but we're remote, so sometimes we don't even know the address. And while all that is happening, the rest of the group has now been triggered.

This was all new territory—there's no book for that. No one has written what the protocol is when a domestic violence event is happening during Zoom. Like a thousand different standards and policies, protocols were being breached here. Confidentiality is being breached, client safety is being breached, and what are the ethics for the counselor to navigate that space? We have no meaningful rules for this situation. There's nothing written in our ethical codes of how you monitor that. If you end that person's participation in the session, what if they are killed? Now there's a moral responsibility to do what you need to do.

So these women were going through all these sessions, in these sometimes extremely difficult situations, and trying to do all the things they were supposed to do to be with their kid, but they weren't able to visit them because of the pandemic. There is a trauma from that, from the tie that's been severed.

Arizona
July 2021

....

Most people who are dying of COVID *have no warning. All of a sudden, they're gone.*

Wendy

Cancer Patient

You know that expression "Man plans and God laughs"? This was a perfect example of it. I was diagnosed two and a half years ago with stage four metastatic breast cancer. It moved into my bones and most recently to my lung. My husband and I were going to take the time we have left together and travel. He retired from his job at the beginning of February 2020, and we took our first trip to Africa. I've always wanted to go on a safari. On the way back, we went to a wedding in New York. When we got home in March, I was deathly ill for five and a half weeks.

Then everything with COVID kind of hit the fan. It was a tough time because we had plans. But then I started looking at it in a different way: *This gives me more time to spend with my mother and with my family.* Sort of. My mother is in memory care, so there were long periods of time where I couldn't go in and see her; only window visits were allowed. Then there was a period where we could just do courtyard visits and it would have to be six feet apart with masks and everything. She has a hearing problem and is a lip reader. Reading lips is hard when a person is wearing a mask. And touch is very important when somebody has dementia, but you have to maintain six feet.

My husband and I, thank God, we get along really well. We've been in the house a lot together. We haven't seen our friends in forever. We talk to them on the phone and that type of thing, but I miss being with them. What I really miss more than anything is playing mah-jongg once a week. I just love it. And I miss playing water volleyball. A group of us have been playing twice a week for twenty-six years. Of course, that sort of went down the tubes because of COVID. Some of my friends and I have been talking about going to a park. We did it once and sat twelve feet apart. But it's hard because some of my friends are just terrified to walk out their doors and be among other people. I'm not.

Maybe one of the reasons I'm not afraid is because of the cancer. In a way—and I know this sounds strange—but in a way, my diagnosis has been a blessing. Most people who are dying of COVID have no warning. All of a sudden, they're gone. They haven't said what they need to say to their families. They haven't done what they've wanted to do. Granted, none of us have an expiration date on our forehead, but I think that in a way I've been blessed with knowing that the cancer is probably what's going to get me. My life span will not be the same as I would have hoped, but it's given me the opportunity to live my life in a different way than I probably would have lived it had I not known.

Arizona
February 2021

There's no point in wearing a face mask if you're going to be tear-gassed.

Breanna

Reporter

I started working as a reporter for the *Indianapolis Recorder* right before 2020 began. It was my first job out of college, and I expected a somewhat easy transition into working full-time in the field. Then on May 6, Sean Reed, a Black man, was killed by an IMPD [Indianapolis Metropolitan Police Department] officer, and within the same twenty-four hours, another Black man, McHale Rose, was killed by IMPD. By late May, after George Floyd's death, my coworker and I were out almost every night covering the protests.

At the start, I would say maybe 90 percent of people in the protests had masks on. The second night of protests following George Floyd's death, the protesters were gassed several times, so masks came off because you couldn't breathe in them.

It was my first time being tear-gassed, and I tried to keep my mask on as long as I could because I was around people. But there was so much pain; it was really hard to breathe. I was terrified and kept wondering, *Will my lungs ever go back to normal?*

The mask absorbs the chemicals and, in my experience, makes the pain from the tear gas thirty times worse in terms of burning your throat and nose. By the time I took it off, I had marks on my skin in an outline around where the mask used to be. The marks were from the chemicals staying on my skin for too long.

After that night, we started to see a lot more maskless people coming out to protest, because there's no point in wearing a face mask if you're going to be tear-gassed.

Indiana
April 2021

You couldn't have that contact, you couldn't
really love back.

Tiffany

Border Humanitarian Coalition Volunteer

Border Patrol brings people here and we help them contact their sponsor or relative wherever their final destination is. We also help with basic needs, like clothing, a meal, and snacks for their journey. Sometimes the families are with us for just a handful of hours. We have a little playroom. It's very simply outfitted, but when the children see it, their faces light up. They are content and feel safe. They know that Mom and Dad are just right outside the door, taking care of business and making those plans for their final destination. The playroom gives kids a sense of normalcy and helps them relax after the trauma of moving from one unfamiliar place to another on their journey, not knowing what's going to happen next.

Our volunteers come in here and play with the children, and we give the kids little backpacks with coloring books, crayons, and little stuffed animals that have been donated. Sometimes the children hug us and we, of course, hug them back.

I remember the first time, it was early in COVID, maybe May or June, when I was playing with a little girl of about six or so and she kept kissing me on my cheek. I still wasn't really used to this mask thing and she was kissing me right where there was no mask or anything. It was so sad because I knew that COVID had changed the distance we had to keep, and that you couldn't have that contact, you couldn't really love back.

Last week, when we were passing out the teddy bears to the kids as they got on the bus, there was a mom who was struggling with the little luggage that she owned. She was trying to grab the luggage, hold another child's hand, and cradle her sleeping baby. I took the baby so she could get the luggage. A volunteer took a picture. When I saw it, I was like, "Oh my gosh, the baby was so close to me." I really don't want COVID to change the dynamic of being able to have contact with the children, but it's important that everyone stay safe. It's just that there are those situations, those moments that you just have to, because no one else will.

Texas
February 2021

*I think it started with me. I haven't quite
forgiven myself for that.*

Jerome

California Resident with COVID-19

When the rules started coming out about wear-
ing masks and social distancing, I thought they were silly. I was one of
the people that said, "No, I'm not going to do this and I'm not going to
do that. It's not going to affect me."

When it hit San Diego, I was still like, *Oh, it's only two people who died,
or people died stubbing their toe, or whatever.* I started to take some precautions, but it was mostly a forced thing because stores like Walmart and
Albertsons were saying you had to wear masks in order to come into the
store. And they were limiting capacity. I remember thinking to myself,
This is ridiculous. This was only supposed to last a few weeks.

In early July, my mom had a serious slip and fall and was admitted
to a neurological ICU in Florida. I started making plans to fly there and
see her. Then I got a little bit of a cough and I'm like, *Goddamn, I'm
going to be on a plane for four hours and I'm going to cough once or twice
and everybody's going to look at me and think I have it.* The cough got
worse, so I went to the VA hospital to get tested. Within a few hours,
they let me know that I was positive.

When I found out I had the virus, I felt ashamed. My boss called
me and she said, "I heard you're out and that you got tested. What were
the results?" I don't know why I lied. I said, "Oh, they're negative, but
I think I still have symptoms so I'm going to go somewhere else and
get tested." I just wanted to delay. I wanted to think about how I was
going to present it because, at the time, I thought I was the only one
at work who had it. A few days later, I texted my coworker and she
texted back, "Oh yeah, I'm out with COVID, I have it." And then I felt
like such an ass.

Why did I lie to her about it? It was this stigma, I guess, that was created around this virus. I eventually came clean with my boss. I said they made a mistake when they first told me, but they got back to me later and said that I was positive, but I'm good now. I took two weeks off and then went back to work. For me, it was like a three-day cold.

Of the eleven employees at work, half of us got COVID at the same time. So obviously we caught it from there. And we gave it to each other. And I wound up giving it to my wife, who wound up giving it to her mom and to her sibling who lived with her mom, and they wound up giving it to my wife's stepfather, who wound up passing away. That was a little tough to deal with because I think it started with me. I haven't quite forgiven myself for that.

California
February 2021

*When I hear somebody saying it was a hoax, I
want to grab them by the collar and say, "My son
is no longer here. It is not a hoax."*

Roy and Kathy

Parents

ROY: In December of 2019, we had our entire
family with us in Florida for the week between Christmas and New
Year's. That experience didn't happen often because one of our sons
lives in Texas, the other lives in Pennsylvania, and we winter in Florida. Getting everybody coordinated and together took some work, but
after that week, I was looking forward to more of the same, maybe
doing something in the summer and Christmas again. Oh, and a trip
to Disney World was in the works because the grandkids from Texas
had never been there.

Then in July, our whole world fell apart. A call that I think no parent
ever expects to get, and when you get it, the bottom of the world just
sort of out falls out. And it's still falling out for us.

KATHY: Our thirty-nine-year-old son in Texas thought he had the
flu and was toughing it out by himself. It happened really suddenly.
On Saturday he was okay and on Monday he was gone. What we know
is that he had some takeout delivered on Saturday. He ate some of it
and put the rest in the refrigerator. He called his wife to let her know
he wasn't feeling well and thought he had the flu. He had Tylenol on
his nightstand and went to bed to try to feel better. He was supposed
to meet some friends to go on a short camping trip, but he never
showed up. When they went to his house late Monday afternoon, he
was already gone. Roy and I didn't know he was sick or not feeling well,
so when we got the call it was, like Roy said, it was the call no parent
ever expects.

ROY: I think part of what angers me is that a lot of the pain people have gone through could have been avoided. In my mind, if people had worked together and treated the virus as a health emergency, rather than a political issue, we would be in a different place than we are today. Both sides politicized the whole thing, and unfortunately, the average person was caught in the middle. And we're paying for it with deaths of family members.

The other thing that angers me is that many people are still saying it is a hoax. I just don't understand or fathom how so many people can die from it if the whole thing is a hoax. When I hear somebody saying it was a hoax, I want to grab them by the collar and say, "My son is no longer here. It is not a hoax. We lost him to a virus that, had we had a unified front as a nation, yeah, there's a possibility he might still have been gone, but not so many people would have been gone and he might have been one of them, but we don't know and we never will know."

But that adds to my pain to think that we're suffering, and a lot of families are out there suffering, and maybe some of us didn't have to suffer.

KATHY: There is a statue, called *Melancolie*, of a parent who has lost a child. The statue has a head, feet, and arms, but there's a hole from the chin to the end of the torso. I can really relate to that because that's how we both feel very, very often. We're trying to find the positives out of the pain and suffering. We've made a pact that we will see our son's children, who are six and nine, every six months. And that's a positive. And we've had discussions with our son who lives a mile and a half from us that I don't think we would have had otherwise.

ROY: One of the things that we didn't realize about our son is the influence he had on so many people. We've heard from his high school friends, his Texas friends, and his colleagues about how he influenced them and had an effect on their lives. We got such nice cards reminding us how much respect people had for him. And it helped us a lot, as it would for any parent, to know that their child had that kind of influence. That was positive for us as well.

KATHY: We've also had some things occur that we can't explain. We keep seeing monarch butterflies. A lot. Where we live in Pennsylvania and where we were in Florida, it was rare to see a monarch butterfly, but I cannot tell you how many times we have seen them since he has been gone. There was one time I will never forget. Ever since he's been gone, whenever I come out of the trailer and look toward the street, I see him throwing the football to his two children, like he did in December when we were all together. Well, this time when I was walking down the steps, monarch butterflies were flying all around me. And the only words that went through my head were, *I'm okay, Mom. It's okay, Mom.* It was just surreal. It was very moving and cheerful.

We have tried so hard to find positives in the whole circle of this.

Pennsylvania
April 2021

*In this small community, when you lose people,
everybody feels it, everybody knows.*

Sherman

Minister

The community my ministry serves went through a great deal of devastation, both financially and emotionally. You have people who were, in many cases, already minimally providing for their families. And now because of COVID-19, hours are being cut, jobs are being cut, time is being scaled back. The funds that they had to have, these resources, weren't available.

There was also the emotional impact. I've lost uncles to COVID-19, I've lost cousins to COVID-19, I've lost friends to COVID-19. In this small community, when you lose people, everybody feels it, everybody knows. I personally know about eight people who died. I think maybe two of them were over sixty. The rest of them were under sixty.

It's made a detrimental impact on my heart as a preacher, as a person who's a spiritual leader. There were funerals where the loved one wasn't even there. It was a picture, like you typically see in a memorial service when something tragic has happened and you're not able to have the loved one there because of the nature of the tragedy. But here it is because of COVID-19. We can't have your loved one here because we don't know if exposure is still possible. You just have this photo. There are a lot of people who aren't fully able to get the closure that they need. Sometimes just seeing gives me closure, that final "Okay, this is the last time that I'm going to see you." And for many, the last time that I saw you was in one of your lowest moments when you were coughing and COVID had its grips on you. It was ugly, and that's some of the lasting pictures that they have.

One of my uncles that passed from COVID was incarcerated, and he died from COVID while he was in jail. We were planning this memorial service and his kids were expecting to go to the funeral home and view the remains. When the remains made it to us, finally, they were not able to see him because things had not been preserved properly. So they did not get closure.

There have been a lot of funerals where hardly anyone was allowed to be there to say goodbye. Mandates were sent to churches and funeral homes saying that gatherings could be of no more than ten outdoors, so no gatherings inside. That was difficult on families because the people that you expect to be there to lean on, they're there, but they're not physically there. So where you would look over and see your uncle or your favorite cousin, and they give you that nod or they give you that smile or they touch their heart to let you know that their heart's going out to yours, that's not there. And those are moments that are part of the healing process.

What I try to focus on is the positive things that COVID-19 has allowed us to do prior to their loved one getting sick. I would talk to them and say, "Well, tell me about what happened." "Oh, well, things shut down and man, we were all at the house together. That's the most time that we've spent at the house together in years." And I would tell them, "That's what I want you to focus on." That's what my faith tells me works. That's what my faith tells me heals.

When I can focus on the fact that whoever you believe the creator to be gave you three, four months of just, "We were together so much we got on each other's nerves." And then from that, they start recalling these funny stories, and these are the stories that bring smiles to their face, and that's where I leave them. I'm not a sad eulogy speaker. I want to leave you on the most positive notes because I believe that the sad things will come. These moments are going to come, but when you can, flash back to these positive moments. Then you're on your way to allowing yourself to heal.

Texas
January 2021

We've not seen as much family togetherness as we do now.

Penny

RV Campground Owner

There has been a huge increase in RVing this year, and it's mostly families. We've owned this campground for over two years, and we've not seen as much family togetherness as we do now. When the families come, the kids don't just sit in the rig like they used to. Now the kids and the families go for bike rides, and they sit out and they have a campfire. I've been really surprised, and I've heard other people say the same thing.

It's one really good thing that's come out of this year, as families have gotten back in touch with each other. Kids have gotten away from the TV because the parents are there to pay attention to them and listen to them, so they don't need that distraction of the TV or video games. I think it's helping kids build more of a relationship with their parents that they didn't really have before. It's a heartwarming part of this year's story.

Nebraska
September 2020

*You can get drunk anywhere. People go to bars
because of the basic human need to connect.*

Michael

Bar Owner

Bars are places that people rely on in disasters.
We're community hubs, a place where people go to be able to contextualize what's going on. So even people who you might not see in a bar regularly, you'll see them in times of crisis because it's a place to get news, it's a place to get out of your house, and it's a place to be around people in your neighborhood or community and reassure yourself that there's other people like you. That things are going to be okay. This particular disaster, though, was one that featured humans gathering as the disaster.

When we had to shut down, we wanted to find a way to be able to serve our clientele. We have a community of people that rely on us to be there for them for whatever reason they need us.

People don't go to bars because they want to get drunk. You can get drunk anywhere. People go to bars because of the basic human need to connect. Given the way modern society is going, there's more and more separation and less and less connection. As grocery stores have gone from local shops to big-box stores, there isn't anyone there to talk with anymore. Same with coffee shops. And now that everything is automated and delivered, you can sit in your home and order everything you need and have every interaction through a computer.

We were very cognizant of the fact that the people that needed us as bartenders were still going to need us, and probably more because they were stuck at home, so whatever drove them out of their house in the first place, that hadn't gone away. And more than that, their social outlet was gone; their community gathering outlet was gone.

We started livestreaming from the bar. We went on every night for an hour, and we did all kinds of crazy things, like we sang karaoke for them, hosted trivia nights, and sometimes made cocktails. I called it a virtual bar, and we were as interactive as possible with people. Sometimes we had guests come on from other places in the country. We ended up building a really, really strong following. Basically, virtual bar clientele would sit at home and have a beer, or they'd have a drink of their own, and they would come and talk to us and they would watch us do silly stuff. We put out a tip jar that they could put money in for the staff. It was surprisingly powerful.

That lasted for a while until Texas reopened again, very early and very unwisely. At the time, we were getting towards the end of whatever resources we had, so we tried to open as safely as possible. That lasted for a couple of weeks until one of my bartenders got COVID. Then I was furious. Furious that we'd been put in the position of even trying to let people in our place. And so, out of pique, I recorded a video that was basically addressed to Greg Abbott, the governor of Texas. It was a plea from a bar in a pandemic. It ended up getting something like half a million views on social media. What a lot of people didn't realize was that bars were excluded from a lot of the aid being offered to small businesses during the pandemic. We were placed in a position of needing to open as soon as we were allowed to, even if it was unwise.

Pretty much right after my video, Texas closed down again because there was a big spike in cases. It was a big spike at the time, but compared to where we are now, it was nothing. That big spike that closed Texas down in July was a fraction of where we are now.

Texas
January 2021

94

*Here in Wyoming, we usually have a breeze, so
even if something were to come out, it would just
dissipate before getting anywhere.*

Sonja

Parks and Recreation Director

We had a great turnout, probably the best we
ever had, for our mud volleyball tournament on August 2. Everyone
was so happy just to get out and do something. We set up the courts
just on the other side of the railroad tracks on some land of the town's,
and we filled them full of water. Everybody parked their vehicles around
the courts, grouped by teams. Weather-wise it was perfect. Usually
in the afternoons we're sent rushing to our vehicles because of some
storm that's blowing through and making havoc, but this year we had
no storm.

Here in Wyoming, we usually have a breeze, so even if something
were to come out, it would just dissipate before getting anywhere.
We felt rather safe. When we advertised the event, we told people, "If
you don't feel good, probably stay home. Use your judgment and be
sensible." At the tournament, I didn't even mention the C-word, just
left it alone. No one said anything and everybody enjoyed themselves.

At the end of September, we had our fourth annual Kite Festival
on the top of our bluffs just south of town. It's a great kite-flying area.
We decided to go ahead with the festival because social distancing is
natural with flying kites. You can't fly your kite right next to somebody
else or your strings get caught up. It went very well.

The drawback to the festival was the fires going just west of Lara-
mie. When I woke up that morning, there was ash everywhere, all over
my patio. More than 325 people showed up for the festival anyway,
and a lot of them wore masks because of the smoke. We gave away
a hundred kites to the first hundred kids and did an "all fly" at noon.

We had kite fliers from as far away as Pueblo, Colorado, and Gibbon, Nebraska, which are both about a four-hour drive from here. Most of them were part of kite-flying clubs. They told us that they were very grateful we still had the festival because it was the only one that was held. None of the other festivals were held. There's usually a big one in Callaway, but because their festival is so huge, their health department didn't let them have it. Ours is not that big, so we were able to do it. The most appreciative were the semipro kite fliers. They were like, "We're so glad you did this. We were hoping you wouldn't cancel."

Everybody's glad that we are doing our events because they want to be normal.

Wyoming
October 2020

I would start by saying, "I'm developing a weird new routine." Now I just say, "Weird new routine."

Aaron

Radio Host

We casually say things now that we never would have conceived of ourselves saying at the beginning of the year.

"Has Orange County updated its tracker of virus case numbers?"

"Another cluster at UNC. Are any of them in the hospital?"

"I have this really awesome face mask; it goes great with my shoes."

Every day, it's another new one of those. Would you have imagined saying any of that when 2020 began?

I made a conscious decision in early March to be as positive and optimistic as humanly possible, even while I am having to go on the air for four-hour local news shows and talk about case numbers and death counts and UNC closing and all of these heavy things. But I also try to focus on how many people are stepping up to help each other and to look at the creative things people are doing to meet the many needs that are suddenly emerging all at once.

What has surprised me is how adaptable we are to new things, new situations. Back in the spring, when people would ask me, "How are you doing through all this?" I would start by saying, "I'm developing a weird new routine." Now I just say, "Weird new routine." They understand. Everyone, as soon as I say it, is like, "Yep, me too."

Everything is completely different now from what it was six months ago, but we've settled into it. We wake up and go through our 2020 day and we look forward to our 2021 day, which hopefully will look a lot more like our 2019 day.

North Carolina
August 2020

Because we've been under twenty cases at any
one time, we never shut down.

Clifford

Gun Store Owner

Every year, our town of Shamrock has a big St.
Patrick's Day celebration. In 2020, St. Patrick's happened the week the
COVID broke out, but we went ahead and had it. Everyone was there;
the town was full.

Now here we are seven months later, and we've only had about
twenty-five to thirty cases total and something like seven hospitaliza-
tions. All recovered, as far as I know, and no one died. Because we've
been under twenty cases at any one time, we never shut down. There
wasn't any indoor dining, though. People aren't comfortable going into
a restaurant and eating.

I can see more and more people starting to get where they want
to get out. They're tired of being home. When I opened my gun store
last week, they said it was the largest ribbon-cutting they ever had in
Shamrock. About a hundred people. It was a big deal because this is
the first new building on Main Street in a long, long time.

We've always been a close community here. The fires of 2006,
which I believe burned up like 1.4 million acres across Texas and Oklahoma, wiped people completely out. I mean, it killed seven people and
livestock by the thousands. It burned down houses and a million-some
acres of grass. When CNN come in here, they interviewed me. What
they wanted to hear about were the bad times, but we take care of each
other here. We always have and we always will. In a rural area, we just
join together. If there's a problem, we all try to work it out. And it's
hard to beat that.

You know, small town America: God, family, and country. We're all here to help each other. We may have our disagreements, but when it comes down to it, we all pitch in.

Texas
October 2020

It's been crazy trying to open a glamping retreat in the middle of a pandemic.

Nicole

Glampground Owner

I feel like I am living the game Jumanji. We've had the stampede and now I'm waiting for the locusts to show up. It's been crazy trying to open a glamping retreat in the middle of a pandemic, but what has made it even crazier is that all my partners and I are healthcare professionals. Three of my partners are nurse practitioners, one is a cardiologist, and one is a practice manager. I am an acute care nurse practitioner, so I do hospital medicine. The hospitalist is the one provider that has to go into the room and touch the patient and do the assessment on the COVID patient every day.

We started the whole idea of a retreat last October. We thought, *Let's build a retreat so we'll have a weekend getaway where we can relax and spend time with our families and our girlfriends.* We started looking for land in Kentucky, across the border from where we work in Virginia. We picked out land in Williamstown, home of Ark Encounter, a life-size replica of Noah's ark. We were on track in March to go to the board of adjustments to get the approvals and zoning and planning, and then COVID happened. Everything was tabled. The governor had shut down the state. Even the Kentucky Derby was postponed.

As you can imagine, no bank is going to lend you money on land that you don't own yet and that you don't have permission to do your project on. We finally got all the approvals in mid-June. When we went to the banks with our approvals in hand, they said, "It's COVID, we can't lend any money. You're a new start-up business and the bottom has fallen out of hospitality." They told us to come back to them "once you all have a couple of quarters under your belt." How do you get a couple of quarters under your belt if you can't get a small-business loan? In any event, we worked around the bank issue by securing a lease pur-chase agreement for the land.

What still puzzles me is why the banks were blind to the fact that our part of the industry, camping, has had 150 percent growth during the pandemic. People are working remotely from campgrounds be-cause they can, and people are camping because they can't get on planes. Demand has really skyrocketed. Before Labor Day, we had a manageable call volume, about ten, twenty people a day. Labor Day happened, people's kids went back to school, and we came back from Labor Day weekend with 100 voicemails. And it's continued. We have been inundated with reservation requests even though our opening isn't until later this fall.

That's another thing: we're opening later than expected because of additional delays due to COVID and a surprising delay due to the wildfires out west. Our tepees from Oregon are delayed because of the wildfires, and our custom sofas, made to fit the units, are delayed because the factories were shut down due to COVID. We decided to still open this fall with a smaller footprint. We were slated to have thirty-six units this year but are going to open with seven and then add in an additional twelve units. So in 2020 we plan to have nineteen units, barring the locusts showing up or a sinkhole opening up in the back of the campground. At this point, not much would surprise me.

Kentucky
September 2020

People are not driving as much—they got nowhere to go. You can't go to the movies; you can't go to the show.

Randy

Auto Service Center Owner

When corona come around, we were worried that we would be shut down because we were a nonessential business. That would leave a lot of folks out there in the cold. I've been doing this for forty-seven years and a lot of people depend on me. They're in their seventies and eighties, and they rely on me to keep their cars going so they can get to the doctors and the druggist and all the things that they have to go to. And then there's the police, county, hospital, ambulance, and prison workers. Somebody's got to keep first responders going. I had my paperwork to justify being open, just in case. Fortunately, I didn't need it.

We are gradually seeing a lot of things change on account of corona, like the parts we buy. Everything is going up for pricing. Not us, our labor hasn't gone up, but a lot of the parts we buy have doubled in price in the last seven, eight months. That has to be passed on to the consumer. Our profits are not in percentages, so my labor is going to have to go up here to compensate for it. I don't think it's really hit yet.

Everybody's taking a year off work, basically. In this business, when you take a year off, you lose a lot of what you need to do your job. I've hired mechanics before and they just said, "Hey, I got a job up here on the farm, I'm going to go do this for a little while. I'm burned out on auto repair." They come back in a year, and they're lost. There's a lot of technology involved in working on a car. We keep up with it every day. If you're not learning something every day and keeping your brain working and keeping up with the times as to what you have to do and how you repair this and that, in a year's time you're coming into a totally new atmosphere. And with this corona, we're having to change everything every day.

We're trying to keep a little bit of social distancing going on. It's kind of isolated now. Each one of my guys have their own little spots where they basically try to stay. We used to go and visit with each other, but we're not even doing that. We also don't get to visit with our customers like we used to, part of it on account of them and part of it on us. I've got a lot of older customers and they're scared to come in. And people are not driving as much—they got nowhere to go. You can't go to the movies; you can't go to the show.

All the gatherings we used to do are all done, even our churches. That's a big issue with me. The Lord said we need to gather and worship, not be separated. It's hard to follow his guidelines and follow the government's guidelines. We have a higher standard that we have to answer to sometimes. You're breaking the law by going to church. But we're breaking his law by not going to church.

I am worried about how people are doing. I can testify that there's a lot more drinking going on just simply because there's a lot more than getting caught. I put Breathalyzers in cars when the state says a person has to have one. Usually it's about a hundred Breathalyzers a year. Here it is only October and it's been 178 since COVID started in March. There's a lot more people out here drinking. That is going to end up being a habit for some of them. This COVID stuff is going to be years down the road. It's going to affect work life, social life.

Arkansas
October 2020

Every single show for the rest of the year was canceled.

Keri

Owner, Canine Stars Stunt Dog Show

In 2019, we were only home in Wyoming for a month. 2020 was supposed to be the same, doing Canine Stars all over North America, from Alaska to Mexico City. We pile our thirteen dogs in the RV and tow a huge trailer packed with equipment. We were doing a show in Florida in February when COVID hit. After that, every single show for the rest of the year was canceled.

When we were home in the spring with nothing to do, I found a great way to use our traveling vehicles. My sister told me that the reservations she works with in southern Colorado had so many stray dogs that people didn't have enough food to feed them. I figured, well, we have these huge vehicles with all these kennels in them and all this space, so I shoved five pallets of dog food from this food bank that had been donated and drove down to the Four Corners area in southern Colorado. I dropped the food off at a couple different food banks, as well as at places where people could get food for their dogs and cats.

Then I took about thirteen cats and ten dogs from the shelters on the reservations and drove them up to Denver, where the shelters didn't have enough dogs to adopt out. While I was doing the transport to Denver, I posted pictures of some of the dogs online. One of our Canine Stars trainers from Illinois adopted one of the dogs I posted, and she started training her to perform.

Things got quiet again after that, with nothing to do. Fortunately, our town of Pine Bluffs invited us to do a show at their annual summer Trail Days Rodeo in August. There were no other fairs or rodeos because Cheyenne was closed down and so was Colorado. We normally would not be able to perform a small, one-day event, so we were really excited to do it for our hometown.

We ended up doing our huge show, like the kind we normally do at state fairs. Some of our trainers came up from Colorado and Illinois because they were so excited to perform again. Hundreds of people came from all over. There were so many people there that all the food vendors ran out of food, which has never happened before. It was the biggest event Pine Bluffs has ever had. Afterward, I thought, *Well, we'll see if there's a big outbreak*. But I never heard of any cases.

You can imagine how thrilled we were to hear from the White Post Animal Farm in Melville, New York, that they were going to go forward with their events in October. We drove our rigs all the way from Wyoming to New York to do it, so we were really hoping it wouldn't be canceled. Even days before it was supposed to start, I was worrying that it would be canceled. And now here we are, doing our shows.

The event, which is limiting the number of tickets it sells, is happening every weekend for a month, and so far the weather has been beautiful and people are spread out and they're having fun. They're just happy to get out. When we first booked this show, I figured that Monday through Friday we would go to New York City, Martha's Vineyard, Maine, visit all these places during the week. But now we're pretty much stuck here. People even told us that it's not safe to go to New York City right now. It's dangerous.

And remember I mentioned that one of our trainers adopted one of the dogs from the reservation? Well, that dog is here at our show in New York. It's pretty cool that none of that would have happened but for COVID. Here's this little dog that was just a stray on that reservation in Colorado and now, because of all this COVID stuff and craziness, now she's going to be here performing in New York. So awesome.

Looking forward, we are lucky that all of our shows that were canceled in 2020 converted the contracts into 2021, so we're already fully booked for 2021. If things start canceling, then it will be time to start figuring out how else we can make money. We've heard of a few shows in early 2021 that have been canceled already, and I'm trying to just not even think about it.

Wyoming
October 2020

If we had to cancel a game in the playoffs, it's unfortunate, particularly if we have the best team in the state, which I think we do.

Josh

High School Football Coach

I've been coaching football for twenty years, and I've been here at Dewar High for fifteen years. I don't like the word "normalcy," but I think that's what football has brought, a little bit of normalcy to life. Especially in Oklahoma, where football is important.

We have a really good football team. Dewar has been ranked highly, usually one or two, in our division. We haven't missed a game, but in our county of six, seven schools, one week we were the only school that played, not so much because of positive cases but because of quarantines. We've had a couple of our players have to quarantine for fourteen days because of contact tracing, but neither of them got any symptoms. One of them was our best receiver.

I'm not saying this in an arrogant way, but we're good enough right now that if we had a few kids that couldn't play, we could still probably find a way to win. At 6–0 right now, I feel like we can win without a few of our guys. But if our quarterback and two or three others get quarantined, we may have to cancel that game. We haven't had to do it yet.

The state association has said that during the regular season, you can try to reschedule and play two games in one week, which they don't usually allow for football because of head injuries and things like that. But they're allowing you to do that right now because of the pandemic.

In the playoffs, though, which start at week thirteen, life goes on. If we had to cancel a game in the playoffs, it's unfortunate. Particularly if we have the best team in the state, which I think we do. We're at week seven this week and the state championship game is at week fifteen, so we're about seven weeks out.

I'm a little more emotionally invested this year because our quarterback is a senior. He has set all kinds of records and he started for us as a freshman. So what happens if, at week thirteen, he goes to grandma's house for Thanksgiving and Aunt Susie has COVID and our principal, who's taking care of contact tracing, gets a call on Monday? Well, he's done. Like, there's nothing anybody can do about it. He will have worked all these years, and he may or may not be sick, and he doesn't get to finish out his senior year. To take that away from him? I don't know how you do that.

Oklahoma
October 2020

*It was going to be difficult for people to figure out
how to virtually teach blind kids to read Braille.*

Karen

Education Coordinator at the National Federation of the Blind

I grew up with a blind mom, and she taught
me the basic skills I needed to learn. But now it's usually the school-
teachers and experienced professionals who teach blind children how
to perform day-to-day skills, like tying their shoes, folding the laundry,
and cooking. Quarantine and school shutdowns meant that the parents
were going to need to fill those roles.

I was a little bit surprised by how overwhelmed parents were when
they didn't have regular support, but it turned out to be a silver lining.
Many parents were very receptive to connecting with blind adults and
learning from them. The parents then realized that they have the ability
to be their kid's first teachers, and it doesn't have to be a professional who
teaches their blind child to make a sandwich or cook macaroni and cheese
or tie their shoes or do whatever. A parent who can teach a sighted kid to
make a sandwich can also teach a blind kid to make a sandwich, especially
if they reach out and ask other blind people. The ability to connect with
and learn from blind adults has been really empowering for parents.

The National Federation of the Blind has done a lot throughout
2020 to reach out and connect people. At the beginning of the pandemic, there were Zoom meetings that blind people could join every
day, providing a gathering space and information about how to navigate
the new challenges.

One of the biggest challenges has been education. Schools went
virtual so suddenly, and a lot of the virtual programs aren't coded to be
accessible for blind students. And a lot of the videos teachers are using
to teach are not accessible. Many of the videos have great, engaging
animation, but kids who can't see what's happening are lost. Videos of

Mentos and Diet Coke reactions are a memorable way to show chemistry in action. But if you cannot see it and there is no accessible written description of what the video is showing, blind children cannot truly understand what is happening.

So the National Federation of the Blind spent a lot of time figuring out how we can teach some of these skills and concepts to blind kids. What we found was, because we designed everything to be accessible from the beginning, the kids were engaged. Because it was designed for them, they could understand what was happening. They didn't have to guess, they didn't have to wonder or ask somebody what's going on on-screen, what happened when we put the Mentos into the Diet Coke.

When the pandemic hit, we knew it was going to be difficult for people to figure out how to virtually teach blind kids to read Braille. Each summer for the past twelve years, we've had what we call our Braille Enrichment for Literacy and Learning (BELL) Academy, two-week programs across the country that are designed to make learning Braille fun for kids ages four to twelve. We figured out that we weren't going to be able to do that in person in 2020, so we started thinking about how we can teach blind kids Braille virtually and still make it fun. So we created a BELL Academy In-Home Edition. This summer, we shipped boxes to 266 participants. Each box contained seven pounds of stuff. We did all kinds of things: Braille egg cartons, Braille puzzles, and we even grew sunflower seeds. We did it all on Zoom.

2020 has pushed me to imagine more of what can be done virtually. I now realize that there's a lot more that we can do virtually than I would have said we could do if you'd asked me a year ago, and blind kids are better for it. We had blind kids who could participate in BELL Academy In-Home Edition from states that haven't had an in-person BELL Academy program in the past, places that have a really small population and a really spread-out population, like Wyoming, where it's hard to pull enough students together for a two-week day program. But we had a kid from Montana participate this time. And so, in some ways, I think 2020 has given more opportunities to some of those more rural families. And I think that's pretty cool.

Maryland
November 2020

You're really going to be angry that I have a mask on?

Luke

Mask Wearer

We have felt more discriminated against for wearing masks than being gay. And that's crazy. In the United States of America, we are getting more nasty comments said to us in a grocery store, on the street, for the fact that we have a mask on than the fact that we're holding hands as two men. That's just hilariously tragic. Like, that's where we're at? You're really going to be angry that I have a mask on? So no shame or foul to people who don't want to wear a mask—just don't call me a sheep because I have a mask. That literally happened to me at the gas pump this week.

South Carolina
November 2020

*Let's take care of each other and try to make this
pandemic survivable.*

Rick

Chamber of Commerce Director

Going into the fourth quarter of 2020, there
seems to be a surge in numbers of cases. Thankfully, we've learned a
lot since the first quarter. I would like to think that even if it got bad
again, we certainly would not ever shut down the economy again like
we did the first time. Of course, nobody in our entire lifetimes has ever
been through anything like this. I understand the concern there, when
they shut it down, but they probably shouldn't have. It's caused more
problems, and there's tens of thousands of businesses that are gone
now that were forced to shut down.

They picked winners and losers. If you were essential, you did
great. If you were nonessential, you had to close your doors. They
should have never done that because it caused businesses to go under
because you called them nonessential. All small businesses are essential because they're supporting families, and that's essential. I would
like to think that even when numbers are increasing we won't see the
economy shut down again.

Now when the governor started to put down some mandates in the
spring, one of them was face masks. And I certainly think face masks
helped. So we started a campaign called "Mask Up Jackson County."
We've done three videos and shared them out on social media. Our
first video was talking about the importance of wearing a mask. We
called it the "Who Do You Wear It For?" campaign. I am not wearing
it for me, I'm wearing it for my grandbabies; I'm wearing it for my
friends that are older than me. In the video, we got a bunch of business-
people, a bunch of local people, to talk about who they're wearing it
for: "I wear it for my grandparents." "I wear it for my grandmother,

who's eighty-eight years old." "I wear it for my sick uncle who's got lung disease." That's who we wear it for.

The theme of the second phase of the campaign was "Who Wore It Best?" We had all these different masks and, again, all sorts of people in the community were in the video. The police chief up in Hollywood wore a mask with a picture of his dog. The third video, done by the high school's videography team, is fixing to come out soon. It's called "Monster Mask" instead of "Monster Mash" because Halloween is right around the corner. We're probably going to keep doing this campaign series all the way through the first quarter of next year, when hopefully things will be getting a little bit better.

So we made it fun, but the whole idea is that it's important that we wear a mask. Let's take care of each other and try to make this pandemic survivable.

Alabama
October 2020

At some point in the pandemic, we were ground zero in the world for the number of cases. The harvest season and the pandemic season collided.

Emma

Migrant Farmworker Nonprofit Director

Our farmworker population start their days at 2:00 a.m., sometimes earlier. Approximately 15,000 to 20,000 of them cross every day, and the lines on the border can be two or three hours long. They leave early so they can make it here in time to get on the bus and be taken to the fields where they harvest the fruits and vegetables that America eats. This area around Yuma is called "America's Salad Bowl."

Our organization provides services to our population, including immigration, housing, parenting, chronic disease prevention, and behavioral health. We're always very busy, so when we started hearing the news that this virus was impacting China and how bad it was, we didn't have a lot of time to think about it. We have a small, rural life, so you don't think a lot about whether something international will hit here. You don't think about how interconnected you are in reference to it. Then at the end of January, we had three cases. It was still not a pandemic at that point, and it was just three cases, so we were thinking, *Okay, so three cases.* We continued business as usual, no additional precautions, just basic hygiene and all that. When the governor issued a shelter-in-place order, we realized this was serious. Shops started closing and people were running around and piling up food and toilet paper.

After our agricultural season ended, a lot of our farmworkers migrated to California, particularly Salinas, San Joaquin, Santa Maria. Then we started hearing about the pandemic hitting them over there, and even some deaths. One man died in a hotel room by himself. The family knew he was very sick. Nobody was visiting him or giving him food or anything, according to the family. The only contact they had was just through the phone, and all of a sudden, he stopped answering. That's how they realized he had died.

During the stay-at-home order, I had a lot of thinking to do about our office here in Yuma. We have thirty employees, and it's important for personal and cultural issues to have direct, one-on-one contact with the individuals we serve. After the two weeks of stay-at-home, we opened the office back up. My husband used to work at the Health Department's emergency preparedness program and helped us understand the precautions we needed to take. We invested a lot of money in plastic safety barriers and hygiene equipment and products, and we had the offices fumigated every two weeks to sanitize them.

Then there was the question of whether to open the doors or lock them and make people knock. But I felt badly for the elderly or the farmworkers who just needed a form to be read or translated or just basic services like that. So I decided that we were going to have to take a risk and open the doors and do whatever we could and pray to God. We were going to face the threats and fight them because we could not be paralyzed; we have to continue serving our population. So we opened the doors. We let people in just two at a time or one at a time to keep as safe an environment for them and for us as possible.

When the agricultural season started back up again in October, the owners of the farms required the workers to wear masks and did temperature checks, but the buses were loaded just the same as before, everyone crowded in. We did two or three campaigns where we went to meet the loading area for the buses at three o'clock in the morning. We provided tote bags with masks, information, gloves, and everything. Our staff was wearing their gowns and PPE, like they were in a hospital. They were there, facing their fears, because what else could we do? One time we gave out about one thousand bags between 3:00 a.m. and 4:30 a.m.

At some point in the pandemic, we were ground zero in the world for the number of cases. The harvest season and the pandemic season collided. Many of the migrants were sick, but they wouldn't say anything. And a lot of them were young, between eighteen and thirty-six, and didn't show symptoms. Migrant workers don't get fringe benefits or sick leave or anything like that, so a lot of them, especially the H-2A temporary workers, didn't want to be quarantined for two or three weeks. So the sick workers wouldn't say anything and then the whole crew would get sick, but they would not say anything. The employers wouldn't say anything either. They wouldn't want the testing to be done for the workers and the workers wouldn't want to be tested, and so there was like this kind of silent agreement. "Don't ask, don't tell, because we need you and you need us." That is what I have been hearing.

Arizona
February 2021

Zoom was really hard because they didn't know what to talk about, so they kept asking "What's new?" over and over.

Dené

Children's Museum Director

Our children's museum has a program called Free Play that provides an opportunity for mothers who are in prison to spend time at the museum with their children. Play is instrumental in strengthening families, and it's the way children process through stress.

We are closed on Mondays, so women who have completed parenting classes and have had no write-ups or problems at their facility can visit with their child here for the entire day. They have breakfast and lunch, they spend time outside together exploring our interactive exhibits, and they do really beautiful art activities. For example, they may trace Mom's arms and cut them out so the kids can take a hug home. We have a photographer, and the kids and moms can have their pictures made. It is very normalizing for the kids, who can go to school the next day and say they were with their mom. We also know that 100 percent of the women say that it impacts their daily choices at the facility.

COVID, unfortunately, has impacted our ability to do the Free Play program. But, just like with everything else we're doing, we've pivoted and we've made sure we could continue that. The program is now called Connected through Play. We create customized learning kits that we're shipping directly to the children, and we tell the custodial caregiver to not give it to them until they are visiting with the mom. We send the mom a guide that shows pictures of what the child will be working with and questions they could ask their child during the project.

One of the things the women told us in their pre-survey was that Zoom was really hard because they didn't know what to talk about, so they kept asking "What's new?" over and over. The response to Connected through Play has been overwhelming. We've all had tears when we've read the letters from women: "We had this really quality visit." "My child felt like I gave them something." "We got to do something together." "I got to be the teacher." So we are able to strengthen their relationships through Zoom visits until we can get them back here in person.

Kansas
September 2020

Renters started coming in droves.

Sharon

Beach House Real Estate Agent

2020 was expected to be another great year for beach house rentals here in Dewey Beach and Rehoboth. And then, boom. We were scared to death. I mean, whoever hears of a pandemic in 2020? It's a word you hear from the early 1900s. With today's modern medicine, how does that happen?

And the first thing I thought of was, *Oh my God, do we have to shut down?* The answer was yes. We laid off the entire staff, including my daughter, who had just come on as a new runway agent. We knew at least that way they would be able to collect unemployment. At the time, we didn't know about the extra $600 a week, which was like a golden umbrella for them. I mean, fantastic.

When March came, it was just Heather and me running the department, which was crazy. The next wave came in April, when the home sales market took off like wildfire. I mean *wildfire*. People started buying properties left and right. We were working seven days a week. Before all this happened, I would have slow mornings. I would get up at seven o'clock, have coffee, read the paper, listen to the news, and mosey upstairs to get my act together for the day, take my shower. All that was out the window. At seven o'clock, I got up, opened the computer, and was in front of the computer all day. My husband would go, "Are you going to take a shower today?" Me: "I don't know, we'll see."

We were going crazy from mid-March until mid-May. I mean, it was just craziness. When we'd have a cancellation, we'd fill it pretty quickly with a new booking. And then they would call and say, "I can't come now because New York just put us in the quarantine." So then we'd have a cancellation again. And then another booking. It was crazy. We did triple the work for the same amount of money, but that's the way it goes. We were so grateful to have the business.

Then the renters started coming in droves. We were already set up for no-contact check-ins, thank goodness, even before the pandemic. So that was taken care of. Renters were, though, understandably curious about how we were making the houses COVID-safe. We all know that the cleaning crews are buzzing in and out every Saturday trying to clean all the houses on their check-out lists. To expect them to comply with all the CDC standards, like disinfecting every single surface in the house and cleaning every single dish, glass, pot, pan, and utensil in the kitchen, was just unrealistic. My husband suggested we hire a local contractor to spray an environmental mist in each house after check-out to disinfect surfaces, all the surfaces. It's environmentally friendly, kills bacteria on contact, and it lasts for nine days. We had them do it on every single check-in. That worked out beautifully, and it gave people a peace of mind. We were the only company that did that, surprisingly. So it all worked out pretty easily. We had the no-contact check-in and the antibacterial spray. It was a slam dunk.

It's a good thing we've got the system down because our season hasn't slowed down. Our September was rocking, *rocking*. We've never had a stronger September and October. And here it is, seventy-four degrees on November 7. Seventy-four degrees for the whole weekend. So the town is hopping. And we've booked more winter rentals than we've ever done before.

Delaware
November 2020

2020 has been a year of change, a year of transformation. It was going to be that for me either way.

Sharen

Amazon Employee

Governor Hogan is on the horn right now, literally at five o'clock tonight, closing down the state again, in November. I remember the first time he did it. I was waiting tables and they cut me early from the restaurant because nobody was there.

All of a sudden, I had a lot of free time. I spent about a week getting my name change process started, watching videos on voice feminization, and practicing it.

Then I saw that Amazon was hiring. Amazon has some of the best trans coverage out there. Some gender-affirming surgeries are covered through Maryland Medicaid, but there are certain ones that are incredibly life changing that are still deemed cosmetic by many insurance companies, like facial surgery that would dramatically increase my safety and decrease my feelings of dysphoria. These surgeries are covered by Amazon's insurance and other big tech companies, like Apple.

So I looked at the Amazon job, and this was back in March when people had no idea how long this lockdown was going to be. I ran out and I started working there, and I've been working there ever since. And now I have access to that care and I'm starting to figure it out. It's really exciting.

Amazon has been really nice. When I got there, even though I hadn't legally changed my name, within a week I had my correct name on my badge, for my login each day, for everything. That was amazingly helpful because I'm at this new job and it's great for new people to meet me seeing my correct name. Transition can be a pretty emotional experience, and living a social life on camera, through our phone cameras, is especially tricky for somebody going through transition. You feel a lot of dysphoria, and it can be exhausting.

2020 has been a year of change, a year of transformation. It was going to be that for me either way. I am incredibly lucky to have so many supportive people in my life, but it's been lonely. Loneliness can feel compounded by being trans, but it has everything to do with being human. There's just this ache, this ache for human contact. To just sit, to talk to each other, to hug.

My hopes for 2021 are to get the gender-affirming care I need and to just be able to connect with other people, be with other people. In a way, 2020 was a little bit of a cocoon for me. I got to be really isolated while I went through some of the more awkward physical changes. And now, along with the rest of the world, I want to bust out and I want to be seen. I want to fly.

Maryland
November 2020

*People's livelihoods have evaporated. All we want
to do is work, but the work does not exist.*

Jennifer

Actor

      Actors are used to uncertainty. We don't know
what our next job will be. We don't know how long the show's going
to run. We don't know if the TV series is going to get picked up. We
don't know if we're going to end up on the cutting room floor. We're
used to not being able to plan ahead. But the pandemic is taking it to
a whole new level.

      I was in a show that was slated to close on March 5. That last week,
there were rumors flying about COVID, about Broadway producers taking steps to possibly shut down briefly. In the dressing room we all said
to each other, "That'll never happen. The show must go on." We never
believed for a minute that theater would shut down. Then, on the following Thursday, March 12, everything shut down. It all happened that fast.

      What has been so devastating are the wide-ranging effects of the
theater shutdown. Yes, actors have been deeply affected, but so has
everyone who works in the theater: costumes, sets, lights, sound, box
office, crew. And everyone else who works to support the theater: the
printers who do the programs, the restaurants who rely on pre- and
postshow diners—it just goes on and on. It is a vast network of people.
And it's all shut down.

      I am involved in a campaign called Be an Arts Hero. This is a
grassroots effort to get Congress to pass COVID relief for arts workers.
Congress still has not passed any additional funding beyond August,
when everything ran out. They still can't agree on pandemic relief,
and it blows one's mind. The arts industry is huge. Arts and cultural
production accounts for $877 billion of the U.S. economy and employs
5.1 million people.

It's not like people in the theater industry are not going back to work because they have unemployment benefits. There is no work to go back to, because theaters are shut down. People's livelihoods have evaporated. All we want to do is work, but the work does not exist.

There have been all sorts of innovations in terms of Zoom and readings and workshops, and I've done all of them, but it's a very poor substitute. What you do in the theater is a communal effort, and it doesn't exist without the contribution of the audience. They're breathing, they're laughing, they're clapping, they're crying. Whatever they're doing, it is a communal experience, and that can't happen right now.

Here we are in November, and things are starting again in terms of film and television. I've got some friends who are regulars on TV shows, and some of those are starting up with extreme protocols and testing every other day. And so far, so good. But theater cannot begin until we have a vaccine.

No one knows how it's going to be distributed. There are a lot of things we don't know. It all comes back to the audience. The audience has to feel safe for us to put on a show. It's magical thinking to expect that we are all of a sudden going to go into dark spaces together in six months. We have to continue to adapt.

New York
November 2020

Amos

Artist

I had been working on completing my paintings for an upcoming exhibit when everything shut down. It's pointless to paint stuff and take it back to the bedroom. You've got to put it out there.

See that tree over there? The one with the CDs hanging from it? I put up a big red easel right next to it and then put different pieces of art out there for people to see. Lynn and I would sit here every afternoon for happy hour and people would walk by, bike by. We met neighbors that we'd never even seen before. And when there wasn't a piece out there, the golf cart would stop or something and the person would holler out, "Hey, where's the work?" A couple of days later, "Ah, you're letting me down!" People were coming by just to see it. It was like living in an art community. Everybody waves when they go by now.

A clown won't perform without an audience, so for me it was a great incentive. And it meant something to people. When it's out like that, it's like fruit on the tree—there's no price on it, there's not anything monetary, it's strictly just what you see. In a gallery, it is more like business, and this is just fun, au naturel. We did it for almost two months. I finally ran out of stuff.

Now everything's online. But anything's better than nothing, right? It's like a musician playing for chairs. It's baloney. At least if you got twenty people, five of them might be sober enough to clap when you finish your song.

I've noticed that some of my friends just ain't painting. I know one guy who's a pretty serious gun. He's got a real job. And I said, "What's he painting these days?" "Nothing. He's got a piece been on an easel for weeks, hasn't done anything to it." I have a female friend who got me started thirty years ago, and she ain't painting nothing. She takes pictures on the beach and posts them every day.

Like I said, the clown won't perform without an audience. It's fun when people like your stuff. It's a lot of fun when people buy your stuff. The stuff that I post on Facebook, that's the only input I get.

South Carolina
November 2020

The nurse would cover me with the blanket and say, "Don't look, don't look."

Ma Luisa

Surgery Patient

We had such a bad time in the quarantine, doing nothing. I met my husband dancing. We love to dance, and we would go every weekend for years and years. When we couldn't do it and had to stay in the house, that was hard. And this year, for some reason, I have been sick with different things, this and that. On November 13, Friday the thirteenth, I felt good finally. I felt wonderful. In the morning, my husband said, "I have to go to the office to drop some things. Don't cook today. We will buy sushi. I have some videos, and we're going to have a good time." I was happy, making plans.

I took the dog for a walk. We were just leaving the park when I heard a door open from one of the apartments, and I saw a big dog running. He was just a big, playful puppy trying to get to my puppy. He crashed into me, and I flew. My elbow hit the edge of the sidewalk. I started to cry like a baby when I saw my arm, hanging down. The pain is the worst thing in my life ever.

The lady said, "Call the ambulance, call the ambulance." I said, "No!" I had seen the statistics. It was the worst week in the hospitals, so many people were sick. I live close by to the hospital, and I see all the time the ambulances. I wasn't going.

I called my husband, and he told me he was taking me to the hospital. I said, "No, no, don't take me to the hospital! Don't take me!" I call to my doctor, and she tells me to go to the hospital. So I went to the ER—my husband dropped me at the door. He couldn't go inside.

One of the nurses put a double mask on me and covered me with a blanket and put me in a faraway corner. This place, it was crazy. Crazy, with people yelling and running. That hallway was the hallway to go to intensive care. Every time the nurses and the doctors come with a patient to take them there, with the oxygen and everything, the nurse would cover me with the blanket and say, "Don't look, don't look. Don't look at nothing." She tried to protect me because I was in shock already. To me, it felt like a nightmare. I looked over there, people dying. I thought, *Oh my God, I am going to get sick and I'm not going to make it.*

When they do the X-rays, I saw my arm was broken bad. The nurse told me, "You need surgery, but we don't have doctors. And we don't have rooms. We're going to put a splint on, and you go and look for a doctor." So they kicked me out with my splint with codeine for pain. It took me ten days to find a hospital to get my surgery. Ten days in so much pain. Finally I went to the hospital for the surgery. It was full of patients. It was the same thing like before—it was crazy. Oh my God. I saw many things that to me, between the pain and the painkillers and everything around me, it was like I was in hell. Like in a nightmare.

I stayed at home for another month. I could do nothing. My husband did everything. Cook, work in the house, clean up the house, everything. He joked with me, "Oh, yeah, I don't do nothing in the house?" One day I opened the fridge, and it was a mess. I started to pull everything out, and he said, "What are you going to do?" I said, "We're going to clean up the fridge. The fridge is disgusting." All these years, he never realized who cleaned up the fridge.

Texas
February 2021

We're all kind of trapped, in a way, because of
COVID.

Gene

Caregiver

For me, and maybe for a lot of people, 2020
became a teaching experience in a "liminal space."

A liminal space is a place where you're trapped. You're in it and you
cannot fight your way out of it. You just have to accept what is and look
at what's coming towards you. I heard that term a long time ago when
I was reading the works of theologian Richard Rohr, who described
being in a liminal space as when you have "left the tried and true, but
have not yet been able to replace it with anything else."

My focus in 2020 was my mom, who was in a nursing home and
had had a major stroke. She was really trapped and couldn't get out of
bed. And she couldn't talk or anything—the visits with her were a lot
of education for both of us—but she could communicate. I marveled
that we'd gotten closer because of her situation. Holding hands and eye
contact was everything, and she was happy to be there with us.

It's interesting to see how we're all kind of trapped, in a way, because of COVID. The more you resist and fight against what has to be
done, the more things get worse. You have to just allow it to be.

It felt that way when the COVID rules were put in place and I was
not able to see her at all. I couldn't sit by her bed and touch her hands
and talk with her. The FaceTime stuff didn't work so well, but at least
there was a caregiver who would contact me when she was somewhat
awake and aware.

We tried to do a window visit, but getting her up out of the bed and
putting her in that chair was just too much. I couldn't go through that
again. I would never make her go through that again.

In May, they called to say she was sick again and they didn't think she was going to make it. They asked me whether they should send her to the hospital or call in hospice. They knew that if she went to the hospital, nobody would be there with her.

That was the toughest decision of my life. I let it sit for a few days because I just couldn't tell them right then. I told them to bring in hospice. But she came back again and survived past May. I'm still not sure she understood why I wasn't coming to see her. Not being able to sit by her and talk to her was really hard.

In October, one of the hospice workers called and said Mama was pretty awake, so we FaceTimed. I've got videos of my mom and me, blowing virtual kisses. She was smiling and she didn't want to let go of the phone. She actually got out the words "I love you." That was the last time I talked to her.

They contacted me in late November and said she had COVID. They said she was going to be put in isolation. Three days later, she was gone. So that was Mom's last year.

Seeing all that and knowing that all these others are in nursing homes, it's just, I don't know. I just can't fathom that those people are trapped in there and their families can't get in to see them. I mean, I understand it, of course, but it's hard to fathom.

I guess it's acceptance.

Odd thing is, in two separate conversations, we were told that COVID had ended her life, but the death certificate says natural causes. I suppose I should get that corrected or at least clarified.

Michigan
January 2021

*When someone dies, we show up, we bring food,
and we hug each other.*

Tina

Grief Counselor

Traditionally, people come together with some-
one who is dying to communicate our care, to express our closing
remarks. That wasn't possible for a lot of people. While some people
were lucky enough to be able to hold up signs or put their hands on the
window for their loved ones to see, many of our hospitals are high-rise
buildings, and you can't stand outside the windows in those places.
And many of our families lacked the resources, the technology, in a
world that suddenly became highly dependent on technology. Devices
became a communication touchstone.

Even though family members were following protocol, there was an
incredible sense of guilt from not being there beside their loved one to
walk with them, breathe with them, as they transitioned from this life.
The chance to hold someone's hand as they transition, that feeling that
they died peacefully, that we could bring our calm into the space and
create this comfortable transition, that was lacking for many people.
There's no way around that; it just was.

Many didn't have the support to come up with new ways of commu-
nicating those unfinished messages or those goodbyes, or those wishes
for peace and comfort during someone's transition. They didn't have
the opportunity to wash the body, to dress the body, to engage with the
body in the same way that is often significant for people in many cul-
tures, and then to have the public gathering of honor, of remembrance,
of celebrating the life. A communal gathering of hearts, of souls, of
stories. I believe memorials and rituals can happen at any time, yet
postponing the celebration of life or memorial for months leaves something lingering and makes processing grief more difficult. All of this

happened so fast that we didn't have a chance to build new rituals and traditions. When someone dies, we show up, we bring food, and we hug each other. But during this time when we're trying to stay six feet apart, we're not hugging. And we are not sharing food, particularly in the early days when we were still leaving the groceries in the garage for some days before even bringing them up into the refrigerator.

At the grief center, we found different ways to help people do smaller rituals: Going outside on their own and floating leaves down the river with the memories that are held. Gathering virtually to read a favorite poem or share memories with others, even if with just one or two other people. Placing an item on a memory table in honor and remembrance and then gathering a few friends to be with you and hold that space, rubbing their hands together as a symbol of "I receive your story, I hold the words that have been shared and the energy around that, and I add my strength and my care to that which has been shared."

Montana
June 2021

It has been so long since we have been all together, worshipping together, feeling uplifted together.

Caroline

Minister

When COVID hit, I said, "Okay, I know what we can't do, but what can we do?" And I've been pleasantly surprised at how much we actually have done. Our church began daily online services, which we'd never done before. And so literally every day there's a service that's filmed. For instance, I do Wednesday morning, the 8 a.m. worship, and people can tune in live. It also goes on our Facebook page, so people can see it at another time if that's more convenient for them.

What's been fascinating is that the average number of Facebook viewers is about 150 a day, give or take. And by and large, that viewership has not dropped. It has maintained itself. And that is what you're going to find with other churches as well. Viewers can come in from wherever to watch, so it's not just Baltimore, it's not just our congregation. It goes out to whoever wants to view it, which is thrilling. That's something to be celebrated.

We also have been offering group and individual spiritual direction, over Zoom and/or outside, in person. Individual spiritual direction has been particularly important because of the isolation and the depressive and/or anxious feelings people are having.

During quarantine, I offered Zoom meetings through our Center for Wellbeing every Monday from 4 until 5 p.m. Four to five is a hard time for some people; it can be very lonely as activities have stopped for the day and dinner has not started yet. The Zoom sessions were a potpourri of humor, TED Talks, poetry, and discussion. Usually, we'd have twenty-five people show up on that. I also started a weekly newsletter from the Center for Wellbeing that had articles about coping, depression, isolation, and mental health issues, as well as links to music, art, and, of course, humor. I had cartoons in there every week.

I have not shied away from talking about hard subjects during the pandemic. Dying, loss, depression, suicide, spouse abuse, child abuse. Fortunately, we had invited our community to start having these discussions in 2019, so when COVID hit, these topics had been normalized to some extent. I just got through offering a four-week miniseries called "The Blessing of Sorrow and the Sacrament of Grief," about dying and death and loss and the unexpected gifts and blessings that can be consequences. If you fully envelop and experience the sorrow, there's potential for great growth.

Looking ahead to the upcoming winter, I know it could be very hard for many people. I recently read a long article about seasonal affective disorder and the prediction that this winter, with the addition of likely quarantines, is going to be more difficult for people suffering from this condition. Staying connected will be key to our mental health, to our ability to find contentment. In one of my discussion groups the other day, a woman who has been an involved, longtime member of our congregation said, "I feel like I'm floating away from church. I need to get reengaged." That is the phrase she used—"floating away." When I think about the winter, I think about how long it's already been for so many places of worship. It has been so long since we have been all together, worshipping together, feeling uplifted together.

Maryland
November 2020

Going to college feels like a privilege.

Melissa

College Student Body President

Our first big event of the year is usually Fall Explosion, when all the students are on the front lawn meeting the different organizations on campus and local organizations. Usually the entire front lawn is packed, but obviously it could not be like that this year, which was kind of disappointing. They ended up separating it into multiple days so freshmen still got to have that traditional experience, just modified. And I think that really sums up this semester, starting off on the right foot by showing students that they still have these opportunities but making adjustments to keep them safe.

In the past, it could sometimes be difficult to get students to attend things, especially on Fridays. Not anymore. I've seen students lined up, down, and around the Pedestrian Mall to get a T-shirt or to tie-dye their mask on a Friday afternoon. It was truly shocking to me because for three years, Friday afternoons were the best time to get parking spots because no one was here, and now people want to be here. Students wanted to experience it to the best of their ability because they didn't know how long they were going to get to be here.

I think, for the first time, going to college feels like a privilege. I went to public school my whole life and my mom was a teacher, so going to school was just what you had to do. But this semester, it really felt like we all wanted to be here. Students wanted to go to class, they wanted to have some sort of social interaction, and they wanted to meet new people.

When it got closer to the holidays, there was a lot of COVID fatigue. Students wanted to go out, they wanted to do things, and I really applaud them for not. I think it made a big difference. Because the day that we successfully made it to Thanksgiving break without having to go online, we were like, "Oh my gosh, we did it!" When I started serving on the COVID Task Force over the summer, I remember that was something we really, really wanted to accomplish.

When we had our holiday event, the Lighting of the Palms, this year, it felt different than any other year. It's always a success. It's always fun, it's always festive. But there was a different vibe to it. I think people were just genuinely grateful for the opportunity to celebrate and be together—safely, of course. There were people who lined up hours before it started because they wanted to attend and they were worried that if it reached a certain amount of people, they wouldn't get to. It was incredibly important to carry on this tradition. It gave people that extra push to make it through the rest of the semester. And I think it gave people some optimism, especially about coming back in the spring.

Georgia
December 2020

We had never done a performance outside on a football field in the middle of a pandemic.

Jenn

Ballet Company Manager

We were still rehearsing, masks on, still acting like we were going to do *Nutcracker*. We were hoping by December it would be okay. But by October, it was clear that we weren't going to be able to do the performance in a school theater, like we've always done. I started looking for a place. We had a few options to be outdoors, and we decided to do it at Yuma Catholic, on their football field.

The amount of work the dancers and choreographers had to put in to just make *Nutcracker* feasible was incredible. We had never done a performance outside on a football field in the middle of a pandemic. Choreography was challenging. A lot of "Oh well, that's not going to work because now we would have to do this, this, and this." They changed choreography daily until they got it to where they needed it to look best to present on a football field, without a full stage. We only had one day to do the dress rehearsal on the field. Our dancers are very well trained and very well prepared, so they flew through that no problem.

From the production side, it was simpler in a way because we didn't have several sets and the usual number of props. We had to nix some things that we normally would do, like having snow falling and fog for the angels. But we had to lay a new floor, get tents, and find carpeting so the dancers did not mess up their shoes.

The stage on the field in the sunshine was wide open, so the kind of magic we like to do wasn't possible. We can't dim the lights to move set pieces. The dancers can't hide behind the curtains and wait for their parts. One of the cool things, though, is that the football field's JumboTron screen was on, which was really exciting.

We had to have an extremely limited audience, with masks and sanitizing and social distancing, all of it. The community said they enjoyed it very much, and the dancers, their joy could not be contained. You could see on their faces that they had never been so happy dancing in their entire lives. They had not been able to perform for almost a whole year. I was in tears. They would have performed for one person or a thousand people—they were just happy to be back onstage.

Now that we know how to do it, we are looking forward to doing more outside performances. We got a grant in 2020, because of COVID, to buy the sports court that goes underneath the dance floor so we can perform outside. Now we can bring performances to the community anywhere.

And now, because of the grant, we can teach anywhere. If schools want to have the whole school come see *Peter and the Wolf*, instead of just the number of kids they can put in the cafeteria or gym, we can perform for the whole school outside in the parking lot. There are so many different, new opportunities we can see.

Arizona
February 2021

You can get all that frustration out right there, on that board.

Caleb

Owner of Axe-Throwing Business

The axe-throwing business has been unexpectedly busy this year. To me, growing up on a farm, axe-throwing started as a hobby. Then I started looking into it more and saw different axe-throwing venues all over the country. In February, I showed my dad a picture of a mobile axe-throwing unit some people were using out in Iowa. He looked at it and, you know, farmer mind, he figured out the dimensions in his head. We started building it around late February, maybe early March, right before COVID shut everything down. I was glad I went with a mobile instead of brick-and-mortar location: we didn't have a bunch of money invested in a location we couldn't use.

Once everything opened back up, our first event was at the Georgia Beer Company right before July 4. That was a big break because they have such a huge fan base. And then things just kind of blew up after that.

Our timing was lucky. People want to have fun, and throwing an axe is a pretty good way to relieve a little stress and anger. I just put that X on the target, and you can get all that frustration out right there, on that board. I guess it went together pretty well with everything that was going on.

It's been a real mess with school shutdowns and the long summer with kids being at home all the time, so there've been a lot of mom groups coming in to throw axes. And I don't know if women have more frustration and rage or if they just listen to the instructions a little better than men, but women tend to be better at axe-throwing. It's true.

There's so much demand around here that I signed a lease for this building, and we're hoping to have a small opening a little bit before Christmas.

And, yeah, we are a little bit worried about having lockdowns coming, but it is what it is. Our employees will be wearing masks, and we'll have hand sanitizer and stuff scattered around everywhere. And social distancing, well, it's something you already have to do with axe-throwing.

Georgia
December 2020

Some part of me knew all of those things were
lies, that the darkness had consumed me.

Dene

Arizona Resident with COVID-19

My wife and I are in our seventies, but we did not fear the virus. We have been vegan for two years, and we eat well, we take supplements, we have a spiritual practice of meditation, and we work out our bodies.

And then we got it. We were down for virtually the whole month of December. It was never really life-threatening, and we knew we had good immune systems that could endure it, but it knocked the shit out of us. I laid in bed and struggled to find the energy to even get up to take a piss. We coughed, we had light fevers, we slept a lot. We each lost seven or eight pounds.

And here's what I noticed about the virus. The virus didn't only attack my physical body; it attacked my mental body, my emotional body, my spiritual body. Its poison impacted all of those dimensions and levels in me. My thinking got very dark; my emotions were very depressed. My spiritual practice of yoga and meditation came to a screeching halt.

I reached a place where I said to myself, *My whole life has been one big lie. I am not who I think I am. I haven't been as loving and patient and kind and compassionate as I have believed I am.* Some part of me knew all of those things were lies, that the darkness had consumed me, but it wasn't until my body began to heal and the virus dissipated that I realized the power of my thinking.

When I'm thinking positively, my body feels positive. And when my body feels positive, I think positively. The opposite also is true. When my body was feeling negative, my thinking was negative, and my body kept absorbing that negativity.

Once I began to come out of that and began to affirm my worth and my value, not only did my body improve, but the whole quality of my life changed. I went back onto my meditation cushion with a ferocity and a commitment like I've never had before. We bought a treadmill, and we converted our spare bedroom into our self-care room, with meditation cushions, yoga mats, and music. We are in there every day.

The virus in some ways was a tremendous gift to us—the ability to recover from that and to reclaim the power of my language, the power of my belief that when I'm thinking positively, my life reflects that. And when my life is going good, all I need to do is say thank you. That willingness to be humble, that feeling of being grateful, changes everything.

Carl Jung said that it is in the darkness, bringing light to the darkness, that our consciousness awakens. I know that to be true for myself because that is what happened in the last two or three months. So thank you, COVID.

Arizona
February 2021

Those activities expose me to a lot of vapor-producing procedures, so PPE would have been helpful.

Sandy

Traveling Medical Speech Pathologist

I work in both the United States and Bermuda. In March, I was in Bermuda because I had taken a traveling position there for my colleague who was on maternity leave. When COVID hit and Bermuda shut down the borders, they stopped all the flights. I couldn't get back to the U.S. The three months of covering her maternity leave turned into a five-and-a-half-month assignment.

To be honest, I was kind of happy that I was set apart in Bermuda. I felt much more protected in Bermuda because they were so strict with shutdowns and masks. There were only four reasons you could be out: to go to the gas station, the bank, the grocery store, or for a medical emergency. And you could only go out on certain days. They even had checkpoints manned by the Royal Bermuda Regiment throughout the island to enforce these restrictions.

The people of Bermuda followed the rules and were very orderly. People wore masks, even at the rally for Black Lives Matter. They don't socially distance so well because, as a culture, they do a lot of hugging and kissing. But particularly in the beginning, they were very, very compliant because they saw all the craziness that was going on in the United States and they didn't want that in Bermuda. The United States was an example of things not to do.

For a while our hospital was out of PPE because the U.S. government stole a whole container ship from the U.K. that was docked in the U.S. on its way to Bermuda. They just took it over. So the hospital did not have any gowns for about two to three weeks. We used patient gowns and scrubbed our exposed forearms like crazy. Masks were worn for several days at a time. Gloves were whatever size you could find.

I spend a lot of time working with patients on swallowing and coughing and talking, and those activities expose me to a lot of vapor-producing procedures, so PPE would have been helpful. It was a scary time.

COVID did come to Bermuda, and my job covering my colleague's maternity leave turned into a job working on the COVID floors. We had about 150 cases total and at any one time we had fifteen to seventeen cases in our little hospital. So we had a lot of COVID cases in the hospital. Right now, we have ten deaths, but we had nine deaths at that time.

I got back to the U.S. in August. I took the first flight back to JFK on JetBlue. At that time, New Jersey was doing better and the COVID cases were going down. I think there was even a point during that August where both hospitals at which I work didn't have an active COVID case. Now we are in a surge, and we have floors of COVID patients in both hospitals. We think it may be a strand that doesn't have a high mortality rate because even though we're seeing a lot of sick people coming into the hospital, they are not dying like they were in the beginning.

You go home weeping, though, because there's so much misery and so much loneliness and so much pain. It's never been like this in my career before. I think it's so hard emotionally because of the loneliness of the people that I see in the hospital. A lot of times I'm in for quite a while with the patients for the kinds of things I do for swallowing therapy and assessments, or cognitive or language assessments.

Patients talk to me about all sorts of things because they don't have that human interaction like they would normally have. They're all alone and nobody can visit unless you're dying. Video chats are okay, but there is something special about person-to-person communication. The gestures, the body language, the touch are all missing.

What has surprised me the most through all of this is the degradation of scientists and science. I just didn't know that people were so antagonistic towards the whole study of science and the study of medicine. Wearing a mask seemed obvious to me. A no-brainer. I was very surprised that people were so vehemently opposed to it.

Through all of this, I've really marveled at our ability to adapt. For Christmas Eve, my eighty-eight-year-old mom likes to go to church.

I said, "Mom, that's great, but we'll do it online because they're not meeting in church." So we go online and we have our beautiful Christmas Eve service and then we get to the part where there's communion. My mom said, "Wait, I want to join communion. I just made some shortbread. I'm going to use that for my wafer." I said, "Well, Mom, you have your Miralax and your prune juice here, why don't you use that?" So for communion, we had prune juice with Miralax, and then we had the shortbread. I told her, "This is a perfect symbol for COVID Christmas Eve service." This is kind of how the year has gone. You adapt, and you move on.

New Jersey
January 2021

My mom's not able to pay some of her bills, but at
least we're alive.

Selina

Texas Resident with COVID-19

The day after Christmas, I just didn't feel very good. On Sunday the twenty-seventh, I felt horrible. They didn't have any appointments available on Sunday, so we got tested on Monday and they told us the results would be back on Wednesday. My taste and smell were gone by Monday, so I knew I had it. I am not a very healthy person, so I was worried that I might have trouble breathing. Whenever I did, I used my CPAP machine and that seemed to work.

My mom didn't have any symptoms until Tuesday, when she got a bad headache that turned into a full-blown fever and chills. She has high blood pressure and she's in her late fifties, so I was scared it was just going to take her out. But my mom's badass, and she doesn't give up easily. We got the results on Wednesday and went straight into quarantine.

In addition to feeling awful, COVID was a problem with my mom financially. She owns her own pet-grooming business, and she does some boarding. She usually made $5,000 in boarding fees for the Christmas holidays, but in 2020 she made nothing for the holidays because no one was going out of town, no one was traveling. So, in addition to having no boarding revenue coming in, my mom also had to cancel all her grooming appointments while she was in quarantine. She started stressing out because her quarterly taxes were due for sales and for federal taxes and she had no money coming in with which to pay her taxes. She's just a small business and usually makes just enough to pay the bills and to survive. Thankfully, I've had my unemployment and that's helped out. Between me buying food and paying the electricity and stuff like that, she didn't have to worry so much, so she could focus on the bills for her shop.

But my mom and I, our experience with COVID was minimal. If you want, thank God, Allah, whoever is out there. We got through it perfectly fine, other than some just-being-miserable days. One of my mom's clients lost his mom to COVID complications, and his father right now is in the hospital in San Antonio in critical condition because of COVID. It affects everyone differently. So, yeah, my mom's not able to pay some of her bills, but at least we're alive. At least we have each other and our friends and our family. We're doing okay.

Texas
February 2021

It's like we instantly screeched to a halt and then ended up getting picked up by a truck named TikTok that was pulling us along at high speed.

Chris

TikTok Star

The start of my 2020 was just about school, auditioning for stage roles, and spending time with my boyfriend, who I had been dating for a while. TikTok was just an app. Little did I know what was going to happen.

At the beginning of the year, I was at Berklee College of Music, going to the Boston Conservatory. I expected to finish out my junior year of college in the spring. I was grateful to have an ensemble role in the school's spring production of *The Drowsy Chaperone* and be in the callback process for a national tour of *Hairspray*. Then COVID came and Berklee shut down and the *Hairspray* auditions were postponed.

The *Hairspray* thing was disappointing, but I didn't feel like I was losing an opportunity, more that it was just getting pushed back. I was more upset and sad about my friends who were graduating and not being able to see them.

At our last *Drowsy Chaperone* rehearsal, we all sat together and kind of cried. We had been so excited to do the show, and it was really hard because no one knew what was happening. We were all kind of losing a thing together. We thought, *Well, we'll be back next year.* They even said they were going to schedule the show for the next year. That, of course, was not able to happen. So many things were not able to happen.

It was a lot of one hundred to zero, not zero to one hundred. The zero to one hundred is coming, though. It's like we instantly screeched to a halt and then ended up getting picked up by a truck named TikTok that was pulling us along at high speed.

The "us" is my boyfriend and me. He and I had been doing long distance, and we were going to be long distance for two more years. Then all of a sudden, we were quarantining together in his apartment in New York City, and we were bored as fuck.

My boyfriend had just come off of a show that they were hoping was heading to Broadway. We both are used to being creative and acting with other people, and yet here we were in his apartment with no creative things happening. My acting class was online, and it's really, really hard to go from a room where you're creative and spontaneous with people to being alone and trying to re-create that.

I wanted to still do something to keep us creative. One night when we were listening to some of our favorite old music and watching a TV show called *Smash* that was on years ago, we started lip-syncing to it. We recorded ourselves and put it on our Instagram Stories. A friend of mine was like, "Just do TikTok, that's what people do there." I had heard of TikTok, but it was a high school app. I thought, *It's cringy, it's not for me.* But then I was like, *Okay, let me open up TikTok and see what it's about.* As I was scrolling, I was like, *Oh, this could be kind of fun. There's a lot of creative things going on in this app.*

The first TikTok thing we did was a fun dance challenge that involved push-ups. It was fitness and dance. Perfect. We got like 3,000 views on it, and I was like, *Holy shit, that's crazy, 3,000 people are watching my video.* And then I remember after about a week we got like 10,000 followers, which was a lot for sure. Those numbers used to be very big to me, like 10,000 people following me.

We were really just doing it for fun. I was still in school, and TikTok wasn't a very big priority, but it definitely has an addictive side to it that's like, *Wow, this is really cool.*

We kept making videos, but there was still that feeling of loss and not knowing what we were doing. Just such limbo. Okay, we'll go to D.C. and stay with my family. Now we're just under my parents' roof again, not very fun. We'll go to Florida; now we're just in Florida, let's go. We had no idea what we were doing—we were just truly wandering. I described it like being nomads the other day. There really was just that sense of being lost but still enjoying our lives and trying to find fun wherever we were.

We started making some of the couple-challenge videos, and the views started ramping up a little bit. In one of them, I asked my boyfriend if we could have a kid. As a joke. I checked later that night, and it started getting a crazy amount of views, like it went from 100,000 to 200,000 five minutes later, to 400,000 five minutes after that. I was getting 1,000 new followers every five minutes. It was like, *Oh wow, this is one big video—we're blowing up, but tomorrow it's back to the drawing board.* The next day we made another couple-challenge video, and that one did the same thing—100,000, 400,000, and then we were gaining 2,000 followers every five minutes. I knew that because I was literally checking every five minutes, because I was like, *What is happening? My phone is blowing up.*

We went from 200,000 followers to 2.2 million. And in that same week, a company reached out to make merch; a manager reached out to start managing us; friends were reaching out from my past; my old therapist reached out to me and was like, "I saw you on my 'For You' page."

We started doing ads; we started making money. I had no idea you could do that. It all happened in about two weeks. We went from doing this for fun to doing it as a job. Then famous people started knowing who we were, and news channels would publish our videos and we would gain followers from that too. Then the Associated Press reached out to do an interview with us. That was wild, because a few weeks after that, every news outlet ever seemed to produce an article about us.

From there we started a YouTube channel, and we were selling our merch. We signed with management, we met with agents, and we've started doing self-tapes for acting roles. It was literally, as I was saying, like we were on this highway and just got picked up.

So what I was expecting in 2020 was maybe do a national tour, maybe get a role at school, and excel in my acting classes. What it turned out to be was to become somehow famous on this social media app, become friends with famous people who I'd idolized, get over twenty articles written about us. I started to make more money off of one ad than I would have made in a year at my minimum-wage job, and I did it all from the comfort of my own home and made like 5 million new friends. So that, in a nutshell, as big as that nutshell is, is what my 2020 turned out to be.

California
February 2021

It's like everything is under glass now.

Sandra

Retired English Teacher

I'm single and I live alone, so a lot my life happens outside my house. When the pandemic hit and the lockdown started, it was kind of a progressive letting-go of the hope that it would be over soon and that I would get back to my plans and to my life.

I am a retired high school English teacher and a lifelong lover of travel, architecture, museums, and the performing arts. The year 2020 was supposed to be my return to big international travel. The plan when I retired in 2017 was to travel whenever and wherever I wanted, and not just during school breaks. Then I fell and fractured my femur. After two surgeries, two rehabs, and two recoveries, I was finally ready to travel again and had a three-and-a-half-week trip planned to Italy, leaving on April 21, 2020. So, yeah. When that was canceled and I was offered a choice of refunds or vouchers, I took vouchers for everything because I wanted to hold on to that plan, that hope, that dream.

I also am an arts maven, so I had a whole season of tickets to performances. I only got to see one and then the whole season was canceled. I had to let go of that as well.

I resisted watching virtual performances for a while. As someone who has been a performer, backstage crew, and an audience member, I've experienced performing arts from both sides. There's just something about the magic and the electricity of waiting in the dark for that chemistry to happen, because each performance is chemistry, just like a classroom. As a teacher, I know for certain that the makeup of that audience changes the performance. I could be teaching the same basic lesson all day long, but it would take on different forms depending on who was sitting in the seats. So that's a big piece that's just not there with virtual performances.

I have watched some virtual performances solely to support the theater companies, to help keep them alive so they will still be around when this is over. Last week, I watched a local company's performance of *Romeo and Juliet*. But I found myself being really critical of the way that it was done because it was basically a film of a stage performance, which is, of course, what it was intended to be. There's a difference between watching something in a seat as a live performance and watching something filmed. When you are in the venue, you can decide what you're looking at. You can see the whole thing or you can zero in on a particular action or person on the stage. But with the virtual performance, the person directing the cameras controlled what I was going to look at. That was really frustrating.

We have lost so much control through the pandemic. This whole process has been not only isolating but alienating. And there's something so alienating about that device being the medium of communication, as opposed to the whole environment.

I found the same issue when I tried to do a virtual museum tour. When you see a museum virtually, it's through the mediation of the device and the decisions made by the director. You don't have the freedom in the experience. You don't have the ability to linger at certain pieces, to decide what you see, how long you look at it, and what angle you approach it from. When I go to museums, I'm sometimes warned by the guards that I am too close, even though I'm not touching the artwork. I like being close enough to look at brushstrokes on paintings and stuff like that. I like to have intimate relationships with the artwork. I see fewer pieces during a visit than most people do, but I visit with them more deeply.

And that is the way I move through the world, the way I interact with objects, experiences, and people. That intimate connection, that individual spark has really been constrained throughout the pandemic. It's like everything is under glass now.

And it's hard to even wrap our head around it, much less communicate our responses to it. But I've felt so much as if I were suspended in time. "Suspended animation" is a term I've used often in my journaling about this whole process and about moments of hopelessness, of *Why even bother? What's the purpose of being here now?* I could easily disappear, like the metaphor of the finger in the glass of water. In the metaphor, the finger displaces the water, but take the finger out and the water reconfigures. It doesn't matter that you were there. I felt like the finger in the water for a lot of this time.

I am not sure how well I would have lasted if I had not found the Auntie Sewing Squad, a group of volunteers all over the country who have been working together, virtually, to sew more than 250,000 masks and send them to vulnerable communities. It was a real lifesaver for me because it created a virtual community and a sense of purpose. But, again, it's artificial in some ways because it's mediated by the screen.

We are very much tactile, face-to-face individuals. So that's still an aching need that is generally unmet in so many ways. I am prone to depression, and I had some really, really dark periods when it was just like, *Why continue with this?* The only thing that's holding me here right now are my animals. Who would take care of them if I weren't here?

California
February 2021

People just wanted to do something normal, like go to a flower shop.

Joanna

Florist

When our governor shut down all nonessential businesses, I had two days' notice to shut my store. I had seen it coming, but I thought I'd have more than forty-eight hours to sell my flowers. I didn't, so that was kind of a bummer. On that last day, I took all the flowers and made arrangements and drove all around the upper valley and gave bouquets to my friends. It was just really fun, so that was actually kind of a cool thing.

It was strange to suddenly have a month and a half off. I normally have two weeks of vacation a year and otherwise I work all the time, six days a week. Some people think, "Oh, it must be nice to play with flowers all day," but it's so much more than that. Having a flower shop is a lot of hard work. You are running a business that involves manufacturing, retail, and service. All at once you're in all three sectors, and you're dealing with a perishable product and emotional purchases. It's similar to the restaurant business in a lot of ways.

So with a month and a half off, I was like, *What am I going to do?* My husband said, "You deserve this time. This is good for you." He's a hard worker, like I am, and we're both Yankees. We grew up in strong families where you don't cry, you don't complain about anything. But he was like, "Yeah, you deserve this, just chill out." So I did. I exercised a lot. I watched a lot of news. And I watched Netflix for the first time. *Tiger King*! I couldn't believe it. I've never seen something so entertaining. I just was sitting on the couch watching TV. I also did a lot of industry webinars and invested in another program to learn some new things.

That downtime gave me perspective on my business that I never could have gotten in a week's vacation. I was able to step away and look at it from a distance in a way that I've never done. It changed my perspective on my business completely. I came back to work with a totally new, exciting feeling and lots of optimism.

COVID was actually good for me and good for a lot of florists. People were home and they couldn't see relatives and they weren't traveling, so a lot of people sent flowers. They also sent flowers to nursing homes, hospitals, and to people with conditions that prevented them from leaving their homes. I also had a lot of spouses who just wanted to support their significant other because they were doing everything, juggling everything, especially parents who were having to homeschool and work full-time. Then when things opened up, people just wanted to do something normal, like go to a flower shop. People came in and they were like, "Oh, it smells so good in here!" So, yeah, just normalcy. I was busier than I've ever been in my life when I reopened.

I lost all my spring and early-summer weddings, and I lost all my graduation functions, but even with that for 2020 I was even sales-wise with 2019. When I got to the end of the year, I thought I had figured it wrong. I don't know how it happened. I'm so freaking lucky.

New Hampshire
July 2021

I thought that if we had a worldwide pandemic and we knew it and we saw it daily, that we would take the right approach.

Mike

Doctor

We have knowledge we learned based on our experiences in past pandemics. Yet, over the last year, we've acted like we learned nothing. That's very disheartening. We have had a lack of direction, and that's been very frustrating. They say that tough times bring out the best in people. It also brings out the worst in people. I have seen benevolence and kindness that was just phenomenal. And I have seen selfishness and self-centeredness that I would never have expected. It's really been an eye-opening experience.

My grandmother used to say, "I've been alive long enough that I have a right to say what I believe, especially if it's true." I'm not even close to her age, but that being said, I also feel that I've been around long enough, and especially around the medical field long enough, more than thirty-five years, that I can be open and honest.

Over the last year, I've become extremely disappointed with people, from leadership all the way down. I've seen political leaders come out and say, "The doctors and the medical experts say this, but I'm going to do what I want to do." And they're supposed to be our leaders. When people say, "I'm not going to follow guidelines because it's an infringement on my rights," I want to ask, "At what point does it become not all about you but all about everybody else and all about society?" Rather than people uniting with a focused approach, which would have led to a lot less suffering and death for many people, many leaders took such a selfish and self-centered approach that it made a bad situation terrible.

And I'll be honest, I would never have foreseen this happening. Previously, I thought that if we had a worldwide pandemic and we knew it and we saw it daily, that we would take the right approach, follow the high road, a consistent approach. We have done none of that.

I work as a hospitalist and do critical care medicine as well as palliative care work. In the Florida panhandle, our COVID hospitalization numbers have been climbing rapidly. From the beginning in March through November, I would have twelve to fifteen patients to work with each shift, with somewhere between two to four COVID patients. Occasionally, I had up to eighteen patients, but that would be a heavy load. On my shift a week and a half ago, I had twenty-six patients, fourteen of which had COVID. COVID-positive patients take about 50 percent more time. So taking care of twenty-six patients was actually like taking care of thirty-nine regular patients. Four of those patients were in the ICU on mechanical ventilators, which takes even more time.

I truly try to provide the best care I can for each patient, but at some point, it's like something's got to give. That is very disheartening to the doctors and nurses and other members of the medical team because we try to give our all, but unfortunately, it doesn't always work. I've taken care of hundreds of patients with this disease, and I've seen dozens and dozens die from it. Yesterday, more than 4,000 people died from COVID nationally. Many of those dying are young, and even more are dying alone.

It's frustrating when the emergency room is packed with COVID patients, the ambulance bays are packed with COVID patients, and we have no ICU beds available for our critically ill patients. I had a patient come in who was not COVID positive, but he was bleeding out from the bottom, terribly, and he had dropped his blood count by two-thirds.

When a COVID patient died, we cleaned the room and then put this guy in there, but he was the only non-COVID patient in the entire ICU. We have other patients coming in who need ICU beds, like patients with acute strokes and severe heart failure. When these patients come in and the hospital tells them, "We don't have any beds, you've got to go to another hospital," that means more time before they're admitted. As they say, every second is brain tissue in a stroke; every second is heart muscle in a heart attack. And we're having to divert these patients because there's no room. And if we can fit them in the hospital but not in the ICU, then they are put on other floors without the equipment and staffing needed to give them the proper care.

I started during the HIV days, so I've been doing this a long time. Now, when I get home after working up to sixteen hours instead of what is supposed to be a twelve-hour shift, I just try to close my eyes, sleep, and let it go. Because I know that I have to go back tomorrow and do it again.

Florida
January 2021

This is not just something we pulled out of the air. The science is there.

Hilary

Vaccine Researcher

I've been doing vaccine research for almost seventeen years. The mRNA platform being used for some of the leading coronavirus vaccines was something we, and so many others, had been studying for years and years. Yet trying to convince my family and friends that the vaccine was real and should be trusted, that was hard.

When family members and friends said, "Well, this hasn't been tested, it was rushed," I would try to explain to them. "This is not just something we pulled out of the air. We have been looking at these for years. I am participating on calls with experts at the highest levels, and the data is there. The science is there."

And yet people would call me up and say, "I know you're sitting in on these calls, but, well, I read this thing on Google, I read this thing on a chat board, and they obviously know more than all these scientists." It was so frustrating.

I believe in science, and I'm not blindly going to go in and say, "You should totally take whatever they want to throw at you." There's real data to back this up, data that medical doctors and scientists were all looking at together, tearing apart, asking questions. Even while we're launching this out to people, we are doing more animal studies to make it better.

Scientists, researchers, doctors signed up to take it as soon as we could to show, "See, we believe in this so much, we trust the science so much that we are putting ourselves on the line, too, as much as we're putting our loved ones on the line."

But it's complicated, and people are complicated. There is so much access to information that is not vetted that folks have a hard time telling fact from fiction, which is making all of this so much harder.

North Carolina
January 2021

David

Local Homeland Security and Emergency Preparedness Director

It's incredible, the parallels between the 1918 Spanish flu and now. Mask wearing, social distancing, closing schools and businesses. They weren't ready for it in 1918, and we obviously weren't ready for it in 2020. The big difference is the vaccinations, which we have and they didn't.

Here in our parish, we practice a mass vaccination every year. It's not just the shot in the arm, it's antibiotics. Within seventy-two hours, we can put antibodies in every person's hand in our area, assuming everything goes like the book says it's going to go. We have volunteer firemen in every community that will go door to door. We don't go door to door when we practice, but we go through where it's going to go, who's going to distribute it.

Here in hurricane-prone Louisiana, we have a lot of experience distributing what is needed at massive scales. We have what we call PODs, points of distribution, that we use for hurricanes and other disaster responses. Water, MREs [Meals Ready to Eat], tarps, water, you name it. If we have to give it out in quantity, we have locations throughout the parish for getting that done.

We have a 12,000-square-foot building here and a 6,000-square-foot building in the middle of the parish where we store our stuff. They're full of PPE right now. Initially, there was not enough for everybody, in no way, shape, or form. I went to our first responders and said, "Guys, it's just not here in the quantity that we need." They said, "What are you asking us to do?" And I said, "Well, the nursing homes and hospitals need PPE more than we do." Every one of them said, "Okay, not a problem." So we started giving our PPE to the people who were on the frontline. Eventually we were able to backfill everything, and we are in fairly good shape now.

I think nationwide, we're right at 400,000 deaths; they were right at 500,000 for the Spanish flu. The CDC is telling us that the vaccine is going to make a dent in the numbers. So we'll just have to wait and see. There's a lot of faith getting put in the vaccine. I will say the vaccine surprisingly has a high rate of effectiveness, compared to the flu vaccine, which a lot of people take at only 40 percent effectiveness.

But a lot of people don't want the vaccine and a lot of people are scared of it. I don't want to have to talk someone into the vaccine. I'm going to just tell them the facts and they decide on their own because it's an individual decision. Some people just say no, and that's their decision.

Planning for hurricane evacuees is kind of like planning for the vaccine distribution. You can ask people in advance "Would you evacuate?" or "Would you take the vaccine?" You have to for planning purposes, so you know how many beds you're going to need or how many vials you'll need. Those are only numbers, though, because people change their mind as things get closer. I don't know what's going to happen, but I think it's going to get crazy when the government says, "Come get your shot." That's going to be exciting.

Louisiana
January 2021

*This virus has just turned everything
upside-down.*

Jim

Grocery Store Owner

Here in southern Louisiana, storms are just
something we expect. I can kind of foresee what's going to happen after
a hurricane and what I need to do to make sure our store continues to
provide what the town needs. But with the virus, it's been completely
different. It's been hard to foresee pretty much anything.

In August, Laura hit as a Category 4. We had over two foot of water
in the store, and it had some damage to it, but it was still intact. We
were up and running the next day, thanks to the Cajun Navy and everybody pitching in. Our store had no electricity, of course, so we ran the
generator every day to keep the store open. The diesel for it cost about
$400 a day, which I was glad to do because people needed groceries.
Like my dad used to say, "I don't know if we're making money, but we're
making friends." Hackberry has been a very good community to work
in. Good, good people.

A couple months after Laura, Hurricane Delta hit. We were in the
center of it.

It's been taking a while to get back up to our regular hours because
our workers are scattered. They cannot live in their homes. Most of
the time when you get water inside, you have the problems of mold
and things like that, so they have to be cleaned out. And some homes
are even torn down. Usually people live in campers nearby while their
houses are being repaired, but this was a tough year to find an RV
because the market was already so hot during COVID. It's just very
expensive. So it's been hard for these people to find homes right now.
They're out of place. Some of them have been driving over an hour to
get to work, from as far away as Lake Arthur.

And the grocery supply disruptions because of COVID have caused problems as well. After hurricanes, we usually need disinfectants and mold killers, like Lysol and Clorox. But because of the virus thing, you just couldn't get them. I called our warehouse, and, because of the storm, I was able to order some pallets of Lysol. I'm all out of it now, though. I keep ordering it and it's not coming in. Anything with the name Lysol or Clorox on it is hard to get. We have other products that don't have the word Clorox on them, and they kill 99.9 percent of germs. So we're trying to get customers to use those.

Even with other goods, the supplies are just not back to normal because of the pandemic. I would think it would start getting better, but there's so many outs. "Outs" meaning the items I have ordered that didn't come in. Like, right here is my paperwork for my most recent order. I have seven pages of grocery items that came in and I have thirteen pages of items that didn't come in. So, yeah, there's a lot of outs, but customers seem to deal with it. And it's not just our store; it's the other stores too. Walmart as well as Sam's can't get this stuff. The strange thing is that there's no telling from week to week which items won't come in. This virus has just turned everything upside-down.

Louisiana
January 2021

Oddly enough, this year did not stress me out. Some of it made me sad, but I was amazingly content.

Anne

Wedding Planner

I've been a professional wedding planner here in Los Angeles for the past twelve or thirteen years. As I've aged, my feelings have changed about the industry, about how much waste there is, about the amount of money people are spending. However, I really love what I do. My niche is to help people have their dream wedding within a modest budget. It's not the kind of job that makes you rich, but I love it, and it has given me a lot of freedom to raise my daughter, to travel, to do other things.

I am fifty-seven, though, and it is becoming harder for me to run around all day in high heels bossing people around, especially if the event is out in the sun. The year 2020 was supposed to be the year when I was going to redefine my business, maybe by doing memorial services or more officiating.

Just about the time I was thinking about the transition, COVID hit, making it impossible for me to do the work I already did, and it also was really unlikely I would be able to launch something new. But as someone who is used to being busy, I had to find a purpose.

I started doing a lunch every Monday in the park behind my house for about ten homeless guys here in South Pasadena. It gives me an opportunity to still fulfill part of what I love to do. I cook, I plan meals for them, and then I go and serve it, and we sit down and have a nice hour together. We picked Mondays because they said that was the one day of the week that there wasn't any place that served lunch or dinner in the area. They go from church to church or different nonprofits in the area to get their meals. It gives me a lot of peace knowing that they have at least one hot meal on Mondays.

As much as I love my job as a wedding planner, and as much career and personal satisfaction I have gotten from it, what I'm doing now is probably the most important work I've done in my life. Oddly enough, this year did not stress me out. Some of it made me sad, but I was amazingly content.

Now that things are starting to maybe open up, I am back to where I was a year ago in January 2020, wondering about whether I want to go full-in on my wedding-planning business or do something different. My financial situation is becoming a little uncomfortable, so I need to figure out something.

Recently when I started posting wedding planner–type stuff on social media again, my activist friends were kind of like, "We totally forgot you had a completely different type of life and work before this happened." So who knows, I may never go back.

California
March 2021

It is frustrating and difficult for many people throughout the world. But that could be good in the sense that it's humbling, and humility is a virtue.

Balarama

Hare Krishna Monk

There are so many ways we can see things. Most people would say, "Oh, I wish it wouldn't happen." The pandemic has been disturbing for a lot of people. But, seeing it from a different perspective, it's a good lesson. I would think at least some people, to some degree, began to realize, "Hmm, I'm not as powerful as I think I am. I'm not as strong as I think I am. Such a small thing as little as a virus has completely disrupted my life, completely disrupted the whole world, and all of my plans and aspirations and everything has been completely disturbed."

It's like material nature saying, "Okay, all of you think you're so big, and then here's this virus and now stay in your room. Stay in your room and you're not leaving." So it's quite embarrassing for the humans. It is frustrating and difficult for many people throughout the world. But that could be good in the sense that it's humbling, and humility is a virtue.

People, they suffer, they struggle, they go through hardships and then: "Well, who am I?" or "What's the goal, what's the point of my life?" or "Maybe I should think of others more" or "Maybe I should try to love people more." Times of struggle can inspire those feelings. And there are people with whom that is happening. But then there are people who are rebelling—"Okay, I'm getting all these signs, but I'm just going to continue with how I've lived my life." Some people, they fall into a deep well of darkness, whereas some people are looking at it as a wake-up call, an impetus to go towards the light.

When the government restrictions came out for religious

organizations, they said gatherings could not have singing or chanting. They specifically said no chanting, which was clearly referring to us. Under the rules, we are allowed to sing and chant as part of our daily practices, but we cannot sing and chant when we have visitors gathering. Having guests visit is a big part of our life here at the temple. In normal times, a lot of people come through here all the time, every day, every week, every month.

Because of the state's restrictions, we were open, then closed, open, then closed, and they did that a few times. Even when it was open, it wasn't fully open. It's now limited to 25 percent capacity, but our festivals and celebrations aren't like they used to be because there can be no singing and chanting. So we're still dealing with that.

Most of the in-person outreach that we would have been doing here has now boiled down to Zoom and platforms like that. We broadcast our classes and everything, but, of course, it's not the same as interacting with people in person. There have also been some worldwide Zooms, like the Kirtan Fest, with people chanting from different places in the world. There were different personalities taking turns, with somebody in India chanting and people from all over the world watching, then somebody in Australia chanting and people from all over the world watching.

Nothing can replace being in person, but there definitely have been a lot of positive steps to try to do something. Despite everything, we have been going out regularly and setting up book tables and passing out spiritual books. In the last few months of last year, monks and congregations distributed 2 million Bhagavad Gitas throughout the world.

California
February 2021

Mike

Restaurant Owner

2020 was my first year that Cafe Italia was making some money. I'm five years in the business, and it takes a while for restaurants to start marking a profit. So, at the beginning of 2020, business was going very, very well. January through April is the peak season, when you really make some money, and then you have to put it aside to get through the summertime. That's how it works in Fort Myers because it's a very touristy area.

But then, March 7, March 8, when it started, the dream of the business doing so well was over.

Most of my customers are a little bit older, and when they heard what was going on, they automatically said, "Okay, we will stay home." But to help me, to keep me open, my customers were ordering takeout at least once a week. And I have to tell you, that surprised me. I never closed—I was open all the time. I wasn't making so much, but enough to pay my bills. I'm very thankful for that. I had a couple of people working for me, but I had to let them go. Me, my wife, and my son, we stayed all the time, and we survived. I am selling lasagna, stuffed shells, spaghetti and meatballs, which is great, and it's easy for people to take home.

I do this job because I have passion, and it's not only the cooking. I love when I see people, they eat the food, and they smile. That's what I love. That's what keeps me going, to make good food for these people. I remember when I was a kid, waking up to the smell of tomato sauce because my grandma used to do the tomato sauce very slow all day. I learned from her. She was always telling me, "Go and get this, go and get that." I would go to the guy who was selling the bread, then to the guy who was selling the mozzarella, then to the guy who was selling the sausage. We used to pay by writing it down on paper. Everyone knew each other. In Italy, when there's a party, you go to piazza in the downtown, you meet everybody. I've always kept that Italian mentality. Food in Italy is part of the culture; it's how you get people together.

My relationship with my customers has become more of a friendship this year. It's like I'm a neighborhood café. I know their names; I might know how they're doing. The couple of seconds or minutes when they come into my restaurant to get the food, the little conversation we have, it grows into a relationship. And after, it becomes stronger. It's not anymore the customer coming in—it's a friend.

So at Christmastime, I gave them baskets of food. It's more of a personal thing so I could thank them. They really came together. They just wanted to help. And then I have another customer who paid for one semester of college for my son. We were shocked. He paid $1,500 for the next semester in school. It was amazing.

I lost about $100,000 in sales, but I know others who lost so much more. I survived to this point, and I will survive the rest. I'm not worried anymore. Everybody needs money to survive, but, you see, my dad always used to tell me, "Money, you can always make it back. It comes and it goes and there's nothing you can do to control it." Friendship, family, that is what you cannot lose, what you must protect. And this is what I'm feeling.

My family and I are blessed. We are blessed that we have a business where our customers think about us. And we survived because of them, and I will never forget that. In a worldwide pandemic, in a business like a restaurant, you have a very little chance to survive. So many are closing and I'm still here. It's just amazing.

Florida
January 2021

*It's January 31, 2021, and there's no indoor
dining in New York City at all right now. It's
been absolutely brutal.*

Dominick

Restaurant Owner

January 2020, business is great, the economy
is booming, life is good. March 15 or so, New York City basically shuts
down. You hear it's going to be potentially two days, two weeks, flatten
the curve, on and on and on.

I am screaming. And so help me, I am screaming, "Protect the
vulnerable, isolate the elderly, isolate our nursing homes, isolate our
hospitals." I was saying this in early March, so help me God. We need
testing, so therefore if you test negative, you can enter a nursing home,
you can enter a hospital. But let life go on—do not cripple the businesses. I cannot be closed for two weeks. I cannot survive being closed
for two weeks.

Two weeks comes and goes. Fast-forward to January 2021. It's January 31, 2021, and there's no indoor dining in New York City at all right
now. It's been absolutely brutal.

Connecticut opened up back in June for 25 percent and then 50
percent capacity indoor dining, and they haven't closed. In fact, they're
increasing their capacity. New Jersey is increasing their indoor capacity
as of now, and Pennsylvania is open again now. So you've got neigh-
boring states that have opened and have stayed open.

The only place that's closed is New York City. And this is where I
get crazy. You can travel basically five miles in any direction and go out
to dinner. I can get in a car and travel twenty minutes to go out and sit
inside a restaurant. In fact, I've done it. You could go to Hoboken and
get a meal. You could go to Greenwich; you could go to Danbury, Connecticut, get a meal. You could go to Long Island to get a meal, in the

same state. I took my son out in Westchester for his birthday, January 4, and we went to a busy, busy restaurant. It frustrates the hell out of me.

I have a restaurant that is starving, all because it's in New York City. So it's just really, really frustrating, opening up Long Island and Westchester and leaving New York City closed. His [Governor Andrew Cuomo's] reasoning was the density of the city, and I understand that, but it doesn't mean that everybody that lives in the city can't go out to eat somewhere else. So he's just crushed businesses like mine.

I just need to be open, and I need the politicians out of my life. Maybe I can never get them out of my life, but I really want them out of my business.

It should be like this: If you want to stay home, stay home. Let the people that want to go out, let them live their lives. Florida is a perfect example. I think Florida is going to be the model that people look back on because their businesses are flourishing. You go out, and there are people in line waiting to get into a club. They have their mask on, they go into the club, they sit down at a table, and they take the mask off, and it's a crowded club. Inside the restaurants, there is really nobody wearing masks. These restaurants, clubs, different types of venues, are just rolling with it, and they're flourishing, economically they're flourishing.

Florida's infection rate and death rate is on par with New York and California, after New York and California have taken draconian measures and, in my mind, fascist measures, to control the businesses and the people of the state. So California and New York are absolutely destroying businesses and people's livelihoods, yet they're right there on par with Florida.

I think the governors and the mayors and the elected officials should step back and look at this. I mean, now it's a little too late, but we are moving forward. Thank goodness we have the vaccine. And you know, God willing, they are saying by June we should all be close to vaccinated if things go really well.

The other day, the governor says, "February 14 we're going to open up the restaurants for 25 percent capacity." There's no science there. It's so arbitrary, so random. But I'm looking forward to opening up on February 14, even if it's just for 25 percent. I have a very dedicated clientele that, thank goodness, cannot wait, so I will be busy. Well, busy to a 25 percent capacity. I won't be making a profit at 25 percent, but I'll have my gears rolling again. The machine will be running again, and that's what's important to me.

New York
January 2021

Libraries were always there for me until the pandemic.

Anonymous

Unhoused Entrepreneur

On January 1, 2020, I woke up in Venice Beach because I had stayed there that night. I was living on the streets. It was a bit eerie the first couple of weeks when the pandemic hit and everything shut down. I was staying out on the east side, and it was weird because there was no one. Everyone took it seriously for the first two weeks, and then all the police were like, "You can't be outside. I'll arrest you." They only said something to me once, and I just kept walking. I wasn't going to argue about it. You can't win an argument. There's no discussion, it's just, you know, do this or do that. So after a few weeks, I realized that everything's going to stay shut down. And then in the summer, I came to Echo Park.

My main goal for 2020 was to keep learning how to program and to start making apps. When COVID hit, I wasn't able to go to libraries anymore, so it has been harder than it was. I used to go to the libraries and work there and, you know, charge my laptop and read a lot.

In 2019, I read probably twenty-five books, maybe more. That's actual books from the library, because I also read a lot of business and economics and finance articles. The *Wall Street Journal,* then Bloomberg and Yahoo! Finance, stuff like that.

I'm telling you, I love libraries. People don't appreciate them enough. Libraries were always there for me until the pandemic. There's a really nice library in Santa Monica, but they closed that one down. I honestly don't know why they can't open them back up and do social distancing in there.

With programming, you have to do it every day, otherwise you lose your skills. It was rough for a little bit not being able to charge. I was

175

having to go all the way to UCLA, Caltech Pasadena, or USC. UCLA is a really nice place, so I go out there to charge often. It's about an hour and a half almost.

I'm working on my first app. I got paid for half of it, so I have to finish it and get paid for the other half. I have a list of like five or six apps that I want to make.

California
February 2021

Jenny

Dog Owner

My dog is almost thirteen years old. I've known her for a long time, but the problem is I traveled for work every week, so she knew me but didn't really know me. Now she is my biggest comfort. When I have stressful telephone conference calls and Zoom calls, she'll just sneak under my desk and try to get my hand on her head to, I guess, relieve some inner tension that I don't even realize I have but that she's figured out.

And I also think my dog is my mentor. She can't communicate orally, and I'm just yapping away. Then there was a moment when I realized, "Wait a minute, I'm just yapping away, she can't communicate orally, but she's telling me something, because I'm talking so much I'm not actually paying attention."

She's more attuned to me than I am to her, so I've learned to become more attuned to her. If not for COVID and this time of quarantine and no traveling, I don't think I would have developed this connection with her. Now she trusts me to brush her. Brushing her every day is one of my key pastimes in our time together. And of course, she wants her treats, right? I mean, the dog loves her treats. That's all she lives for it seems. And then she also has trained me to give her dog food every day at a certain time of the day. She will look at me so that I get it for her and she follows me to make sure I put in the right number of cups. It's our bonding time, and that is one of the things I treasure.

Virginia
March 2021

I moved into a part of the house that was separate, and for fourteen days, we got to see each other through a glass.

Ted

Entrepreneur

During the holidays, we already were getting word from people we knew that something was happening in China, and the advice we got was "Cancel whatever plans you have for February, March, April. Just cancel them all."

At the end of February, I have a friend who was reaching a milestone birthday about the same time as me. My wife with our friends organized a surprise guys' twenty-four-hour trip to Las Vegas to celebrate both of our milestone birthdays. There were about ten people on a 200-something-seater plane. It was an epic time.

To continue the celebration after Vegas of my upcoming fiftieth birthday, a weekend celebration was planned, with people coming in from all different places. I remember that Wednesday before, we were down to the wire. We've got to make a call whether we're going to cancel this thing. Thank God we did, because that was the weekend when everything went nuts and people were in the stores stocking up. And it turns out that several of the people who would have come to the celebration were just traveling back from various places, and the next week they were sick like crazy. They didn't know what it was, they just knew they didn't feel well. We would have had the second major superspreader story in Los Angeles if we hadn't canceled.

At this same time, my mother-in-law, who has compromised health, was in town visiting. We put her on a plane back home to Canada because we were concerned the borders were going to close. Thank God we did because when she arrived back, Canada started restricting flights.

It felt like we were always one or two steps ahead of what was going to happen because of keeping abreast of what was going on in the world and just trying to make the smartest decisions to keep from really disrupting our lives and getting sick.

When I realized I wasn't going to be able to travel, I had to figure out how I was going to stay integrated with the companies and projects and teams we have all over the world: Mexico, Japan, London, New York, L.A., Washington, etc. I usually clock 100,000 to 150,000 miles a year. Fortunately, we had been working a lot through videoconferencing for the past year. So I set up multiple videoconference stations in the house, some stand-up, some sitting, because I had the sense that this was going to last for a while and I couldn't imagine being stuck at the same monitor, in the same location, day after day.

In April and May, I was starting to have all kinds of foot problems. It turns out that shouldn't have been a surprise. I was having twelve to fifteen hours of videoconferencing every day, standing up and walking around barefoot on a carpet. No wonder my feet hurt.

Ironically, I've probably never been more busy in my life. People and organizations were willing to consider things that they wouldn't have done otherwise, and that opened up so many possibilities. I missed being able to visit them in person and go out for dinner and drinks and all that, but at the end of the day, I think the relationships got a lot deeper because we were collaborating multiple times a week, every other week, and we didn't have to wait for when I'm getting on the plane. With everyone doing videoconferencing instead, it became much more fluid: we could talk anytime, and people were a lot more accessible. That was the beautiful part of it.

My wife, who is an actress and in film production, cannot work remotely. The film industry was pretty much shut down in Los Angeles because there were so many protocols and complications that you could not rely on getting a complete shoot. A lot of productions started heading up to British Columbia. It's only one of a few places in North America that has been able to shoot. Fortunately, my wife is Canadian, so she was able to go up to Canada in July and continue work. She's been up there ever since.

Before she left for Canada, we had never been apart for more than five days in the seven years we've been together. We constantly videoconferenced, but that was not the same, of course. When I finally was able to go up and see her, I had a fourteen-day mandatory quarantine, with up to a million-dollar fine if you broke it. I moved into a part of the house that was separate, and for fourteen days, we got to see each other through a glass but not actually be together. During that time, she went on a film shoot and there was an incident, so everyone had to self-isolate for five days until everyone on the team got tested. So, between the fourteen-day quarantine and the five-day self-isolation, we had to wait nineteen days before we could be physically in the same room.

Now I am heading back up again tonight because Canada is about to put in new restrictions that will require a hotel stay even if you've tested negative right before your flight. You have to test when you get off the plane and wait for your results in a government hotel, which they say is going to cost at least $2,000 or more. If you test positive, then you get to spend a lot more money, upwards towards $10,000 or more from what I am hearing. I got my test yesterday, but I didn't want to chance something going wrong, so I also took a rapid test on Monday, just for a sanity check. So I'm heading to the airport in a couple hours. Fingers crossed. I am not sure when I'm coming back home.

Texas
February 2021

We're scrappy. We were going to figure out a way.

Vincent

Creative Agency Cofounder

Sometimes you have to just show not only yourself but the world that "no" doesn't mean it's over. Our company, Concreates, deserved just as much of a chance to survive the pandemic as any other small business, but the government didn't agree. It said we weren't worthy of getting a PPP loan to pay our employees because we were ex-felons.

Things had been rough for creative agencies like ours because as soon as lockdown happened, there were no live productions or shoots, so advertisers were using user-generated content instead. They didn't really need us for that, so when the PPP program was announced, we were super hopeful that we would get some relief. Then we were shut out because there was a provision prohibiting loans to companies with owners who had criminal records.

We teamed up with the ACLU and Defy Ventures, and we sued the Small Business Administration. They had no right to put that clause in the law. It's disaster relief, which our taxes pay for, and we pay taxes. And most of us who have served our time turn to entrepreneurship because it's so hard to find employment. To penalize our company, our employees, for a crime committed decades ago that had nothing to do with the pandemic, that's just not right.

The ACLU won the lawsuit and the government changed the clause, but we still never got a PPP loan. Even on this second round, we still haven't gotten it yet, but we expect it will happen in the future. The category for our agency, which is advertising, isn't in the drop-down menu and it's causing all kinds of issues. Anyway, that's been super crazy. All these other companies got PPP so they could pay their people so their people could eat.

My team and I, we're scrappy. We were going to figure out a way. When the murder of George Floyd happened and all the protests and national discussions were going on, brands started to realize, "Oh, we do need their voices." Some of the biggest brands in the world began coming to us, and some of our agency partners brought us into discussions with some of their biggest clients. That's how we have been able to sustain ourselves in terms of revenue, but we had a production issue because a lot of our team freelancers are behind bars.

When COVID first started, folks in prison were dying at a high rate, right? We lost a couple of our guys to COVID, and some got sick and then recovered. Some of our people got released on compassionate release because of COVID. And our process as a team, working together from the outside and the inside, got way messed up because the mail from the prison was really, really slow. Also, they weren't allowed to go to the computers. They were all quarantined and you couldn't really check in on your people. But we are scrappy, and we made it work.

Fast-forward to now. This is my last day on federal probation, and the future's looking super bright. Every day that we wake up, we get to start over. As long as you've got breath in your lungs, you've got opportunity.

California
February 2021

I drove my sister home to Connecticut to drop her off and I didn't leave for three months.

Celia

Documentary Director and Producer

On January 1, 2020, I moved into my apartment here in Brooklyn. I was going to take a break in 2020 because I didn't have a lot of work on my plate, and I had not taken a real vacation since 2017. In March, I took my seventeen-year-old sister to Disney World. The place was still packed, and my sister ran around Lysol-wiping everything while I rolled my eyes, convinced she was overreacting.

I think we were on one of the last full planes back to New York. I drove my sister home to Connecticut to drop her off and I didn't leave for three months, because the next day Trump declared COVID a national emergency, everything shut down, and the bottom fell out of my industry.

I am twenty-eight and I have not lived with my parents for fourteen years. It was a trying experience every day. But it's true when my mom and other parents talk about all this extra time they got with their grown children that they never would have gotten otherwise. When else in our lives have we had an experience that every other person is going through as well? We didn't have a choice; we couldn't go do something else. So we spent time with our families and looked to do all of the things we'd been putting off for so long. Whether those things actually got accomplished or not, I don't know. I've heard that lots of people cleaned out their basements.

A real silver lining for me was that I got to live with my sister, who is ten years younger than me. I left for boarding school when she was four years old, so she has no recollection of ever living with me. It was great to be with her. We did a lot of paint-by-numbers, baked banana bread like everybody else, and did every stupid tie-dye kit, every kind of thing like that, to pass the time. And I got to hang out with her while she went through part of her senior year of high school.

I'm not good at being unproductive, so I really struggled with that. Looking back, I should have enjoyed my downtime more. I would give anything to go back to that for a little while.

Ironically, 2020 was probably my busiest year. I started work at about 8 a.m. and stopped work at about 1 a.m., six to seven days a week. It is not good for your mental health, I will tell you that. I do not really sleep. But it's absolutely a coping mechanism: work was the one thing I could control this past year, and so I dove headfirst into it.

As we begin to come out of the pandemic, I'm finding it hard to get back to a place where I have a normal work-life balance. The lines have blurred so much that it's hard to know where work ends and your life is supposed to begin.

One of the things I talk a lot about with friends is that we will have gone into COVID at twenty-seven and come out at almost thirty. People my age have lost years of potentially dating, getting married, and having kids.

There was the thought that maybe the pandemic would push people to date more or to become more serious about finding a partner, but I think it's done the opposite. We've lost so many of our social skills, and I think we've also lost some of the desire to date. Dating is tough anyway, and the past year has made it even more difficult.

New York
June 2021

*The rites of passage that normally help people
with ending and beginning different phases of
their lives did not happen.*

Shabnam

New Mom

I've always been very driven, and I was never
interested in being a stay-at-home mom. And yet here I am, having
spent the past seven months, 90 percent of every day, with an infant.
On January 1, 2020, there were three big changes happening in my
life. First, I was pregnant with my first child and had not told anyone
yet; I was still early in my pregnancy. Second, I had just given notice at
SoulPancake, the company I helped start twelve years earlier. Third, I
was planning to take a one-year sabbatical to figure out what I wanted
to do next.

SoulPancake's mission is to create uplifting and inspiring content
about human connection, but in building this company about human
connection, I became disconnected to many people in my life because
I was working eighty, ninety hours a week. In fact, I felt very disconnected from everything.

I've worked every day of my life since I was sixteen, so I was excited
for this year off. I had a lot of grand plans for the six months before my
baby was due, including trips to reconnect with family and friends, a
Hawaii babymoon with my husband, a dozen speaking engagements
all over the country, and, hopefully, meetings and coffee dates with
about 150 people I wanted to talk with about the next chapter of my
career. None of that happened.

As I got closer to having the baby, I felt this pressure that time was
running out, and I struggled with a lot of questions around my identity. The rites of passage that normally help people with ending and
beginning different phases of their lives did not happen for me. There

had been no SoulPancake goodbye party, so there was no closure to a decade of my life. There had been no baby shower, no celebrating the coming baby with family and friends. On top of that, there was doctor-required bed rest that confined me to my couch for the four weeks leading up to the birth. I went from being an active executive, managing a large team, building something, traveling three to four times a month, to being on a couch and having to ask for help for everything in a world that looked completely different. It was a really hard time.

Then an injury during childbirth immobilized me after the baby arrived, and because of COVID, we needed to keep the baby sheltered until his immunity built up. My feeling of isolation was profound. And coming from a very big Persian family, I had expected that I was going to have this baby and he was going to be handed off to my village of fifty people every single weekend. Instead, he spent most days in my arms.

But my husband said something that made me think. He told me the whole world is basically home with an infant right now; it's not just me that's feeling these feelings of isolation and missing out on milestones—everyone is experiencing a little bit of this. It helped. While I was simultaneously feeling incredibly insignificant, but not in a bad way, I was also acutely aware of how I'm just one person among 7 billion living in my little plot of land in the world, that I am one drop in the very large sea of the human family.

It has been in this time of being alone with my son that I have found something so surprising. I have become quite focused on the little things and how powerful little moments can be. It has made me far more present than I've ever been in my entire life.

Because I've always had so much going on, I've never been squarely in a single moment. I am so present and in tune with my son that I know when he's tired or hungry or wants to play with one look. I never would have thought that I would find any fulfillment in being a stay-at-home mom, but on many days, I'm happy just being with him; he brings me so much joy. I still hunger for doing impactful work and contributing to the world, and I miss that, but I find fulfillment more often than not in the day-to-day, which I never expected.

I think I lost a lot of my previous identity. I was an executive, a creative producer, an entrepreneur, a keynote speaker, an author. All these were aspects of my identity, and I lost a lot of them without any fanfare. It just happened. And so I felt a lot of grief, sadness, and dis-appointment, and I went through a period of fog. That's the only way I can describe it: I was just in a fog for the two months leading up to the birth and after the birth of my son.

In the five months since I've come out of the fog, I've found an appreciation of the small circle of family and friends that I think is most significant in my life. I believe we all have this circle: the people who matter to us and to whom we matter. I realized that we over-estimate our self-importance and our significance in the world. I think in understanding our insignificance, we can find real meaning in and connection with the people closest to us.

And I've also realized what I want to do next in my career needs to be meaningful, because if it's going to take me away from the little boy that gives me so much meaning, it has to be a powerful contribution to the world. So that's the last year of my life.

California
March 2021

These kids live out in the middle of pastures for days, and they don't get any reception at all.

Jennifer

High School Teacher

I had heard of the virus, but I never thought it would get as far as Mississippi. The week before spring break, it still had not even dawned on me that this was going to affect me and my students. Then I heard that some schools might be closing down or extending their spring break. But I thought, *That won't happen here.*

When our high school shut down and went virtual, we had no way of actually going virtual. We're a Title 1 school, so it's not like our students had computers.

They had all the teachers come in and make these big, thick packets with materials and assignments for the kids to work on at home. My question was, "How are we going to get these things to everybody?" We live in a very rural community. So in the back of my mind I'm thinking, *How long can this go on with the packets?* Not only do you have to come to the school drive-through and pick up the packet, you also have to come to the school drive-through to drop it off and pick up another one at the end of each week.

At first we had a great turnout. We had parents picking up for their own kids as well as for other kids in their neighborhood, because the kids' parents were working and couldn't get there. The first packet was due within a week, and the kids did a great job on that. The second packet was due within two weeks. The next one was due within two or three weeks. The response rate really had faded off by that time. The kids just weren't turning them in. And teachers were concerned about whether the packets had germs on them, so they would let them sit for days.

We did the drive-through pickup about three times total. And really, that's how school ended. Over summer break, I joined a Facebook group called Teaching during COVID-19. It was a lifesaver because teachers from all over the world connected with problems they were having. There was a lot of sharing about how to use the different platforms, like Google Classroom, Blackboard, etc. We also were able to answer questions for one another about little strategies along the way, like how to keep kids' attention when they are online instead of in the classroom.

When school got ready to start at the beginning of August, we were told it would be held in person but with everything available virtually. The school system knew we might have to quarantine some kids or maybe even go all-virtual if the number of cases got too high, so they started us out doing both—in person and virtual—right from the beginning.

It was full mask, and everybody was scared to death at that point. We were disinfecting all the time. Everything in our classrooms had to be disinfected between classes. When you have eight classes a day, like we do, that's tough. Then, to monitor exposure to other students, we were required to have seating charts for every class and to turn the charts in to our assistant principal. We were told the kids had to sit in their assigned seats and not move. Whenever a student in the class tested positive, the nurse would come into the class with a tape measure, seating chart in hand. She would walk over to the desk of the student who was positive and she would measure six feet around it. Whenever a student was within six feet, she would say "Gone." Just like that. It was so weird.

So kids were sent home and had to keep up virtually. I was wondering how I was going to teach Senior English when my kids didn't have Chromebooks at the start of the year. We had been begging to get enough Chromebooks for the kids in time for the school year, but that didn't happen timely, of course, because everybody in the United States was ordering Chromebooks and iPads and whatever they could get their hands on.

Ninety-nine percent of my students had cell phones, so that's how the year started. And us teachers were just kind of thrown into the online platform that we were using, which was Google Classroom. Students were learning from each other, and I was learning from them.

The teachers were told to put an assignment online every day for virtual students. Eight assignments a day times five days a week means forty assignments a week. We weren't supposed to use paper for the assignments, even though we were in person at that point, because the school system was worried about the transmission of germs on the paper. As you can imagine, doing forty assignments a week was difficult for students who were using their cell phones as their online devices. It was even more difficult, of course, for students without cell phones or Wi-Fi. When we finally got our Chromebooks in October, everybody was fired up until the kids got home and couldn't get any Wi-Fi reception.

In December, hotspots arrived, free of charge, for students to take home. The problem is, so many of these kids live out in the middle of pastures for days, and they don't get any reception at all. They can't get reception on their cell phones, so they're not being able to get it on hotspots. For the most part, the hotspots were kind of a joke. We even had teachers who could not get Wi-Fi at their houses.

A lot of my students took the opportunity of virtual school to up their hours at work—McDonald's, Wendy's. About half of my 106 students work, and in many cases, they were working jobs to support their families. I can't tell you how many of my students would be doing class virtually while they were driving down the road to work or out back behind their job, taking a break. They would log on as much as they could.

We were told that as long as students did their daily assignments, they would be counted present for the day. And in my class, nothing was marked as late. Maybe I'm too easy, but nothing was late because our group of kids, most of them were poor and they're working to support their household, at eighteen. It's crazy.

I am passing all my seniors. One of my students went through a tubal pregnancy this year and lost the baby. She missed a lot of assignments, of course, but I'm not going to be the one to tell her she can't walk across the stage during a pandemic.

Mississippi
March 2021

*Everyone could relate to the chaos of working
at home, with kids jumping over your back and
talking to you while you're trying to work.*

Chris

Monologue Writer, *The Tonight Show Starring Jimmy Fallon*

Jimmy's last in-studio show was Thursday, March 12. Without an audience. That weekend, Jimmy told us he was going to do the show from home. "I'm going to work from home like everyone else," he said. And we're all like, "Awesome, yes, we're doing this!" Then in the next breath, it was like, "How are we going to do this?" But all credit to Jimmy: he set up a tripod, made a TV show, and basically shot from his house. And it kind of took off from there.

As a writer for the show, the first thing I had to figure out was, *Where do I even work from home?* I had a one-year-old and a three-year-old in a small New York City apartment in Queens. There's not a lot of space, so I have been working in bed. I've been in bed ever since. I joke that it's like the grandparents in *Willy Wonka.* I'm sitting upright with my legs out and I'm typing away to the sounds of the chaos going on in the next room.

My days have been basically working during the day and trying to keep two toddlers entertained throughout the week. We tried all sorts of things, from pool parties in the bathtub and to obstacle courses around the apartment. It's fun until our downstairs neighbor left a nice passive-aggressive gift of two kids' padded slippers on our doorstep, which is kind of a nice way of saying, "Keep your kids quiet." Like, do you understand these are two toddlers in New York, so there's no keeping them quiet? One of the things that was great about Jimmy's at-home shows was watching him interacting with his daughters. It was just real, and everyone could relate to the chaos of working at home, with kids jumping over your back and talking to you while you're trying to work.

A huge challenge of working from home has been that I miss the camaraderie of the writers' room, where there was always someone you could turn to and ask, "Is this funny? Can you help me? Is there a rewrite here?" Yes, you can bounce ideas off fellow writers in the Zoom box, but everyone's on mute. Pitching jokes out to silence is really uncomfortable. It's probably something like what Jimmy was experiencing.

You'd write material for Jimmy, he'd sit down and tell jokes to a tripod. Even though you knew there wouldn't be laughter, there was always a heart-sinking feeling every time there was just dead silence after a joke. Maybe his wife, Nancy, would chuckle, or maybe the kids wouldn't laugh, and that made it funnier. But seeing those jokes die to silence every night was hard. You just had to tell yourself, "Maybe someone at home found that funny."

We wanted to make people laugh and give them something to look forward to at the end of the night. People were having a hard time, and they wanted a show that was an escape from what was going on. As a writer, that posed some difficulties. How can you escape from the pandemic when everything going on in the news was about the pandemic? So you felt like, while you wanted it to be an escape, you also had to talk about what everyone was going through. And I think that's where our team sort of geared towards—what was on everyone's mind at the moment, whether it was panic buying of hand sanitizer, mass wiping down of groceries, people working over Zoom. We were writing for an entire new world.

Another challenge was writing our weekly bit that we call "Thank You Notes." They've always been my favorite part of the show to write for because you can write about anything, and that broadness is what is exciting, especially for me, who writes about the news every day. Observational humor is fun and different. Usually you find inspiration for it when you're just out and about, living your life, taking the train, walking by people. But how do you find inspiration when you are working from home, especially working in bed? When you're just looking around your room for the 100th day? Thank you, blinds. Thank you, ceiling fan. You just kind of lose all that sense of the outside world in a weird way.

It's an exciting time now for the show to be in front of a full audience again. When Jimmy walks out there and he says, "I can feel the love," you really, really can feel the love of the audience. He's just so pumped. It's exciting to see him read your material and hear the audience laugh. Finally.

New York
June 2021

The COVID *Queens, that's what we're called.*

Amy

Pageant Competitor

When we arrived in Vegas for the pageant at the end of March, the city had just opened up to 50 percent capacity indoors and people were required to wear a mask at all times unless they were eating or drinking. If you were in a dining area but not eating at that particular moment, you would have to put your mask on.

I was coming from North Dakota, where our mask mandate had just been lifted and all of our bars and restaurants and schools were open. And I was vaccinated. So arriving in Vegas was like being back in March 2020, when the pandemic first started. It was crazy to me to see how shut down the state was still.

Finding places to eat in Vegas was difficult because most staff people had not returned to work. You had to make a reservation, and if you didn't, you weren't going to get in. A lot of places weren't even open, and it was really hard to get around in Vegas because Lyft and Uber drivers were still not back to work. Some of them didn't feel comfortable, and some were just like, "Hey, I'm getting my unemployment benefits still, so why go back to work?"

The Mrs. America organization did a wonderful job in keeping us safe by adhering to state guidelines. They ran three pageants at the same time, which meant a total of 153 contestants, and to my knowledge, none of us contracted COVID.

We wore masks the entire time, even when we were competing onstage. The clear Mingle Masks we used made it tolerable. They actually look pretty darn good—I was pretty amazed. They did a really good job of showcasing our face while keeping us safe.

We did get to do the pageant in front of an audience, even though it was limited in size. At first, we didn't know if we were going to be able to have any of our family or friends come watch us. So it was great that we each were allowed four tickets. One of the highlights of the Mrs. America pageant is having your husband walk you across the stage, which we didn't know if they would allow this year. Fortunately, they did.

The silver lining is that we still got to compete during a national pandemic, which is amazing. The COVID Queens, that's what we're called.

North Dakota
April 2021

There was grief in that we couldn't connect in the
ways that had given our lives meaning.

Katie

Mother and Friend

I struggle with anxiety, and this year was like nothing I've ever experienced in terms of my own personal anxiety. I started out the year happy, in a good place with my home life and my work life. Then everything we are drawn to in this world in terms of connection was suddenly potentially fatal. Everything was completely upended. I was going through grief, fear, worry: worry about my parents, worry about my children, worry about myself, and worry about my business.

Watching my happy kids be sad, away from their friends and school, was hard. I have a second grader and a fifth grader, and there was an emotional toll on them. My youngest child has an autoimmune disorder that had taken five years to go into remission. So we didn't see people in the way that we had.

We were a very social family, so we went from being in the world, being social, being in community with people, to being with the four of us. From being out in the world and having our own things that we did every day, to being on top of each other.

Home used to be where I re-upped my energy, but over the past year I never really got to re-up at home. That's been really challenging for me, just finding space to be alone. There were times when I would just go drive around or sit in my car in the driveway. There was no getting together with friends over coffee; everything was closed. There was grief in that we couldn't connect in the ways that had given our lives meaning.

Fast-forward to today, my forty-first birthday and my first day of being fully vaxed. It feels like a rebirth. One of my really good friends is taking me out to eat inside a restaurant for my birthday. It's my first time eating inside a restaurant in fifteen months. I do have some anxiety about it, but I trust science. I'm just super excited that we are getting out in the world again. Until my kids are vaccinated, though, my anxiety is still there.

This has been the hardest year of my life, but I've also probably learned the most about myself and what matters this year too. When my husband asked me recently what I wanted for my birthday, I said "I want letters from my friends." So he coordinated it, and I got like twenty-five letters and photos from some of my best friends this morning. I was overcome with emotion and it was just really cool. That's all I want. I want to be with the people I care about.

Minnesota
April 2021

I have done half of my sophomore year and all of my junior year at home.

Joanne

College Student

When UC Berkeley announced that school was going to be online, my housemates and I decided there was no point in paying Bay Area rent to be taking online classes, so we've all been at home this year. At first, we all thought it wasn't going to be that bad, and we were all like, *Oh, it's just like a break from school.* But as it goes on, you realize it's not really a break, and the semester gets worse and living at home isn't always the best situation. I think all of my housemates have had issues adjusting with their family and parents. In the beginning, we were all optimistic. As it went on, we got less and less optimistic about everything.

For me, what I miss is being able to hang out with my housemates. Sometimes it's nice when you're studying to just turn around and there's another person there to talk to. When I'm home, it's just me. My family is all very introverted, so they're fine with quarantine. They're all in their own rooms, doing their own thing, and I'm like, "Hey, let's all hang out together." And they're like, "No."

I've pretty much had nothing else to do except my classes. My summer internship didn't work out because it needed to be in person, so I even took classes during the summer. In July or August, I came across Pandemic Professors, a nonprofit that provides free online tutoring to low-income students. I am an education minor. I applied and started tutoring a third-grade girl.

It's been nice to be able to see her every week and bring a sense of normalcy to her life. As a third grader, it must be tough taking online classes and being stuck in your house. It was just really nice to be able to do something to help someone and still kind of feel like my life is in order because I'm doing something to take control of the situation I'm in. In addition to tutoring, I'm now interning with Pandemic Professors too as the head of "Tutor Success." So I'm helping out a lot behind the scenes with the tutors, which feels even more like I'm controlling what's going on in my life because it's more of a commitment.

Pandemic Professors isn't something that would have normally happened. I feel like I found something that I really enjoy doing and something I want to continue doing even past the pandemic. I guess I would say that I found a deeper purpose. I've always wanted to do education, but now I think I solidified that a little more. And working with nonprofits and education is something I've really enjoyed doing right now and that I think I want to continue doing.

I am still at home, taking classes online this spring. So I have done half of my sophomore year and all of my junior year at home. I cannot tell you how much my housemates and I are looking forward to going back to Berkeley for the fall. We are so excited! We're apartment hunting right now, and we've created a whole bucket list of things we want to do before we graduate.

California
May 2021

A lot of it, especially in the beginning, was almost surreal.

Jim

Food and Agriculture Company Chairman

This whole COVID pandemic has been a learning experience. Every week it seems like we learned something new. For example, as we learned that temperature checking was important as a way of distinguishing who might have the virus, we quickly moved in that direction. Our purchasing department, when there were no thermometers around, figured out a way to get them, and we had them in here by mid-March. We have 21,000 people around the country, so monitoring temperatures was critical. Then, a few weeks later, when we realized that spacing between people was important, we put in Plexiglas and plastic barriers to try to isolate people as much as we could in their jobs in the plants.

When someone's temperature read high or people thought they might be sick, they could go to the Wellness Center at the plant where they work for further analysis and advice about whether to go home and quarantine. We are very fortunate that we've had Wellness Centers in all of our facilities for years. They are staffed by nurses and frequented by doctors from the local community who see workers by appointment, right there at the facility at no cost to our associates or their children. Our Wellness Centers became a really important hub during the pandemic.

Our plant associates and truck drivers came into work every day, notwithstanding the virus. They are essential workers for sure. We increased their pay and gave everyone the usual profit-sharing bonus at the end of the year even though we didn't actually earn it because of our increased expenses due to COVID. And when workers said they couldn't grocery shop as easily, we provided chicken products every week to them to take home. We also donated food in many of the communities where we have operations, as most of them are very rural communities that do not have a lot of infrastructure, including, in some cases, grocery stores.

Keeping up with the health needs and COVID-prevention requirements for our workers all over the country was a challenge because each state had their own guidelines, their own health systems. We brought our former chief medical officer out of retirement to make sure we had an experienced expert at the helm. Dealing with different health departments became a very, very important part of our job, including my job. I was assigned to different states' health departments to talk about what they were recommending, what they were learning, and what we were learning.

For example, one of the big learnings we had was that just because an area did not have any positive cases did not mean it was going to stay that way. For example, we have a plant in North Carolina in a very rural area, and they really didn't have any positives until midsummer, which was quite a ways into the pandemic. Then, all of a sudden, our doctor said, "Keep an eye on the community. If it starts going up, you're going to see positive cases in the facility." And that's exactly what happened. So a lot of the communities' onset of the virus sometimes was delayed, but eventually it seemed to get pretty much everywhere over time.

Another thing we learned was that what people were doing while they weren't at work was really important. One example was carpooling, which, of course, was something we had always encouraged in the past. During COVID, though, carpooling became a real problem. At work, people would wear a mask, a smock, and their caps. When they were done for the day, they'd throw their masks away, get in a car together, and take off. So we tried to encourage people not to carpool or, if they did, to wear their masks. Again, this was part of the learning experience.

When it came to contact tracing, we started finding there were different communities of workers that had more issues than others. By doing that tracing and analysis, we were able to take the whole group and say, "Please stay home for ten days"—or, at the time, fourteen days—"and don't come back before that. We'll pay you for the whole time. We think it's better that you don't come back to the plant until you're tested."

Of course, testing became a big, big issue. We did 100 percent testing at several of our facilities, and actually, the positive rates at our plants were always less than the surrounding communities. I think that was due to the learning we were doing, and how we were trying to avoid the positive rates in the community spreading into our plants. That is a lot different than some of the rhetoric that people were hearing, which was just the opposite. But again, that's part of this learning process we're going through.

When the vaccines came out, that was the next challenge because a lot of people didn't want to get a vaccine. So we worked with Johns Hopkins School of Public Health, which has a group that educates people about getting vaccines. That's what this group does. I think most of their work is in Africa and other places where they're trying to administer vaccines, but their experience was essential and important. They provided us with materials and encouraged us to set up tables at our facilities and tried to answer questions to make people feel more comfortable about getting the vaccine. To this day, we have plants that are about 60 percent vaccinated, and we have plants that are around 30 percent vaccinated. And so, that's still an ongoing challenge. The question is whether we need to incent more people to get the vaccine. Because, ultimately, the vaccine works, and it stops the spread once a certain percentage is vaccinated. So that's another key learning that we had to go through.

Personally, the times of my highest anxiety throughout the pandemic were in the beginning and height of it. We were doing all we could to try to protect the health of our people, but it was still scary. A lot of it, especially in the beginning, was almost surreal. There's really something to be said for stability, and there wasn't much of that for a while.

I learned from my dad long ago that we are in the people business. He would say that you could be making tin cans instead of chickens and it wouldn't make any difference. It's all about who has their hands on that product. They are clearly essential, to not just Perdue, but to the continuity of America's food supply, and I'm so proud of them.

Maryland
June 2021

It's not all that gratifying to be singing alone in your home when you're used to singing with 100 other people around you.

Pam

Choral Conductor

Zoom is great for many things, but singing together is not one of them.

I am a choral conductor for several choirs, including the Cambridge Community Chorus, which has about 130 adults from ages twenty-one to probably eighty-five. We normally present two major concerts during the year, one in December and then one in May. In December of 2019, our Duke Ellington concert was so packed that we got in trouble with the campus police because we were breaking fire codes. We'd never had so many people before.

When everything shut down in Boston that Friday, the thirteenth of March, the executive officers of the Cambridge group and I got together on this cool new platform—well, it was new to me—called Zoom. We brainstormed ideas about how to keep people engaged and making music in creative ways.

Zoom, though, wasn't the solution for us that it was for other organizations. Because everybody's internet and lag times are different, you just can't sing together in real time. For example, if a bunch of people are on Zoom trying to sing "Happy Birthday" together for a friend, it's a disaster. It's just one simple melody, but it's a mess. So imagine trying to sing things in four or five, six parts with 100 people. It's not very good. At all.

For the first rehearsal, I decided to do short little rehearsals for each group of singers, the sopranos, the altos, the tenors, and the basses. I sat at the computer and sang their parts with them and played it on the keyboard while they sang along from home with their headphones on.

All they could hear was their own voice and me singing, no one else. Some of the singers were pleased that we got to rehearse our music. But then at the end of the evening, after three hours of very careful planning on my part to keep them engaged, somebody said, "Oh, this is so frustrating, I can't do this. I'm just going to sit out for the rest of the semester." It was so deflating because he was right. It's not all that gratifying to be singing alone in your home when you're used to singing with 100 other people around you.

So we got creative and found new ways to keep our community connected musically and socially. We had over eighty people participate throughout the past year, choosing either voice classes, music history lectures, or singing choral music. About thirty-five of them wanted to keep singing repertoire, even if they couldn't hear each other in real time. So I learned how to use GarageBand and Soundtrap. They recorded themselves on a device, then sent it to me so I could sync up all the parts. When we put it together, it sounded like a piece in real time.

In October, we had a mini-concert and played the recordings that we had made of those thirty-five singers. That night, when the group heard the music come together for the first time, it was amazing and very emotional. People were crying. As we came into December, we created an audio recording of carols that we sent out to assisted living facilities in the Cambridge area where we usually sing around the holidays. Then in May, we put together a spring concert of both audio and video recordings.

We had to learn a completely different way of doing things in the past year, but we stuck it out and made beautiful music. It was very rewarding. But, as our members have noted, when we do come back together, it's going to be so much more magical to sing in the same place and experience the joy of making music together.

Massachusetts
June 2021

The COVID pandemic gave some of the poorest an opportunity to say hello to their children.

Nikia

City Leader of Individual and Family Supports

A lot of times when people talk about the pandemic, they are like, "Oh, it hit the reset button for people." For the people in deep poverty, it was an opportunity for them to have a chance just to sit down for a moment and breathe without having to worry about who was going to care for their child, how they were going to pay their light bill, how they were going to make their rent, how they were going to do this, that. Before the pandemic, individuals and families were working so many hours, working two or three jobs, they didn't have a chance to really even understand what their kids were doing in school. They didn't know where their kids were, what their kids were doing, because they were constantly working. They were just hoping that the schools and teachers were doing what they needed to do to get their kids to that next grade level.

I know this from supporting the VITA free tax-preparation program throughout the city of Philadelphia. Philadelphia has the highest deep-poverty rate among the country's ten largest cities. Deep poverty is people living on less than $12,000 a year for a family of two or more. Those same individuals that came into the tax program last year with two, three W-2s that added up to less than $15,000 a year made over $30,000 receiving unemployment payments plus the stimulus in 2020 because of COVID. They had a chance to breathe. And quite honestly, you talk to some people in the hood or people that are impoverished or in a challenged situation, and they'll tell you, "COVID was good to me."

I have two sisters that make $14,000 a year. Yes, they work. They work all the time. One of my sisters works from 11 p.m. to 7 a.m., and during the pandemic she's working 2 p.m. to 10 p.m. She doesn't have a chance to think about her daughter because when she gets home she's tired, she sleeps. And she wonders why her daughter falls behind a little bit. My other sister, before the pandemic, was living with me because she was making so little. Since the pandemic, she has gotten her own place, she's been working, and she's caring for our mom. When her car went bad, she used the stimulus payments to buy a cash car. Yes, it has 180,000 miles on it, but it probably could go another 80,000 miles.

These are individuals that were making beds and working in hotel rooms for ten and twelve hours for $7.25 an hour, or working in the restaurants hoping they could wait enough tables to make it work. You cannot live on minimum wage, you cannot raise a family on minimum wage, without working second and third jobs. The COVID pandemic gave some of the poorest an opportunity to say hello to their children, to understand where their children are in school because they had to homeschool them or do virtual schools from home. One woman said to me, "I never had sat down to have dinner with my children until the pandemic hit." One of the children was sixteen years old.

The COVID break gave people an opportunity to think about how they want to live their lives. It's given parents a chance to sit down and understand the children they are raising. Our children are our greatest natural resource, and if parents don't know who they're raising, if they aren't putting up guardrails and they're not setting the tone, then our children are poorer off for it. COVID gave some of the poorest individuals an opportunity to get grounded and go back to being more family oriented and deciding, "Hey, I want to be better, I want to do better."

A lot of people will say that these people are lazy, that they don't want to go back to work. What is happening is these people are just reassessing. They are tired and they need to have jobs that pay enough to meet basic needs like food, clothing, and shelter. That's what they want, and that's what we should give them. The pandemic has proved that direct cash payments do help people thrive. They buy better food, they take care of their children, they keep their lights on, and they put the money to good use.

Pennsylvania
June 2021

Training for the outsized endurance test that is a triathlon is not unlike what was happening for us as doctors during COVID.

Carrie

Emergency Physician and Triathlete

In the last few weeks of February and beginning of March, I was literally on six different planes, traveling to Orlando, San Diego, back to Florida, and then home to Boston. In early February, there had been inklings about a virus that was coming out of Wuhan, China, but we really didn't know very much about it at all. I was going on with my life. We started to have our first couple of COVID patients trickle into my emergency department in downtown Boston, and we realized very quickly that the world was shutting down. That first month was overwhelming, all-consuming, and there was so much uncertainty. I am responsible for training the 750 interns, residents, and fellows at the hospital, so a big part of my job was thinking about how to keep them safe, how to give them the proper protection, how to help them navigate this new disease, and all the things that were completely changing around their training.

I have a son who has congenital heart disease, and I knew I was taking a risk going into our respiratory care unit every day. So I sent my son to live with my parents in a remote part of Maine for three months. I think it was just very acute for all of us, that personal sacrifice you were making to be a frontline worker. At the same time, there was this great, deep sense of purpose. We had a field hospital open up for the homeless called Boston Hope, and I signed up to work on providing critical care there because I thought, *When else in my career is there going to be a field hospital in my own city?* I needed to be a part of that.

As we got to the summer, we realized how much this was dragging on and that we were getting worn out and tired. For me, travel had been my way to recharge so I could be more present as a single mom for my kids, as a doctor for my patients, and as a leader for the doctors I was training. Now that travel was no longer a possibility, I had to figure out how I was going to continue to show up for the people in my life who needed me to be strong and present and patient and thinking. What I found I needed the most was to build some physical strength, some vitality, some goals. I needed to build myself up in a way that I could show up as my best self. A friend mentioned a trainer, Nelson, who had been working with her son. I figured, *This is a good chance to get in shape.* When Nelson and I met, he asked me what my goals were. I said, "I have this really incredibly important work, which the pandemic just amplified, and I need the strength and vitality and capacity to handle this better." Over those next four or five months of COVID, I lost thirty pounds and gained a lot of strength.

It seems like COVID created this space in which we would say, *What story am I going to write now? What's the story of my life that I want to see moving forward for me?* It also seems like COVID created space for us to stop and think, *Who do I want in my lifeboat as I am going through a crisis and who do I want to fill my life with?*

With Nelson's encouragement, in March I decided to do the New York City triathlon in July. Swimming in the Hudson for one mile, bike twenty-four miles, and then run through Central Park. The first time I was on the bike, I lasted about fifteen minutes. Swimming, I lasted about ten minutes. Slowly, every day I got stronger, and I started to see myself as a triathlete. As I thought about this year and all that had happened and all that had been, the triathlon felt like the perfect way to put a capstone on all of it. Training for the outsized endurance test that is a triathlon is not unlike what was happening for us as doctors during COVID. The first time I did my open-water swim, about a month ago, was this moment of, *We've made it; we're going to be okay. And look what I can do now.* It reminds me of all that we went through in the early parts of COVID and then the long haul of COVID.

A lot of the things I was used to in my life before COVID have fallen away, but this whole new identity has emerged. I think that's my wish for everyone. As we're coming out of COVID, we have things that we

lost, but there is something new, too. Some new dream or some new
identity or possibility that you haven't had a chance to try.

Massachusetts
July 2021

My doctor said, "There's a new strain of COVID, *and I think you have it."*

Amanda

Wisconsin Resident with COVID-19 Twice

Ironically, 2019 was a lot like 2020, and 2021 has been even worse. In May 2019, I caught a virus that made me really sick. The doctors don't know what the virus was, but it stuck with me and I had all these complications afterwards. I was homebound.

By the time 2020 arrived, I started to feel better. I was like, "2020 is going to be my year of health!" When the pandemic happened, it was a flashback to everything that happened to me in 2019. I've always been a super positive person, so I was one of those people who was out there writing inspirational quotes with chalk on people's sidewalks. To make people smile, I put a giant inflatable unicorn in my window with rainbow lights.

I have a baking business called Amanda Cupcake, and I wear a pink wig and do all this fun stuff. I was making videos and sprinkling sparkles on cupcakes. I was just trying to make the best of a dark situation. That was my way of coping with it.

Yes, we were quarantined at home, like the rest of the country, but my daughter and I were having so much fun. Like right now on my Timehop app, I keep seeing all the activities I did for her every day during our 2020 quarantine. We made an animal-themed miniature golf course out of cardboard boxes. We taped toilet paper rolls together and made slides for her dolls—the dolls would slide into a cake pan full of colorful pom-poms. Even though there were times when I was scared and I was sad, I just kept creating things.

I remember New Year's Eve 2021. I was celebrating with a friend over text; we were actually in tears because we were so happy. We were like, "We've made it through something that was really, really difficult."

And for me, I had made it through not one but two really difficult years that seemed very similar to each other.

Then 2021 came, and it has been harder for me than 2020 was. I'm not the same person, and that's okay.

Right at the beginning of January, I had all these ambitions. First of all, though: I live in Wisconsin and I hate the cold, but I knew that we were going to be stuck inside a lot because I am a stay-at-home mom. I was like, "I'm going to be the fun outdoor mom this year. No matter how cold it is, we're going to go snowboarding, we're going to go sledding."

My daughter and I went to my parents' house, where there's a steep hill. My daughter was having a blast sledding. My dad came out to see her, and I'm like, "Should I go down?" I got in the sled, and it went really, really fast. I tipped over and crushed my hand on something. It was my right hand, which I use to create, to design, to make cupcakes.

That night, I sat on my couch with my husband after we put our daughter to bed and just cried. I was so sick of everything being canceled. I had been trying so hard, and breaking my hand just felt like a big slap in the face. But then I thought, *I can do this. I have to be strong through this.*

Two days later, my husband started coughing. Two days after that, when I started to get a dry cough, he got his results. All three of us, my husband, my daughter, and me, had COVID. My daughter got over it really fast. My husband and I kind of battled through it. I had different symptoms every day.

On day six of COVID, everything on my skin started to burn. If you even touched me, it hurt underneath my skin. My doctor said it was a cytokine storm, but he said that since it was mild and it went away, I would make it through.

I kept my doctor informed about what was going on because I have a history of medical problems that doctors don't understand. I'm a mystery case. I'm only forty-one, but I have a loop recorder in my chest because of A-fib and other heart issues.

On day nine, I lost my taste and smell but didn't have any respiratory symptoms until the next day. It felt like I couldn't breathe. The doctors told me it probably was because the passageways were inflamed. They gave me an inhaler.

After about ten to twelve weeks of recovery, my hand was finally out of the cast and I was ready for a new beginning. I started exercising, doing some spring cleaning, just getting back to normal.

Then all of a sudden, I started to feel really tired. This was like April 13, about ninety days after I tested positive. I still couldn't taste or smell but decided to get blood work done because something wasn't right. I also thought it could be depression. I had started losing my passion for things ever since I had covid. I started feeling numb, and that's just not me. I couldn't even come up with a new recipe as Amanda Cupcake.

My doctor said, "There's a new strain of covid, and I think you have it." I didn't believe him. I was like, "You've got to be kidding me. Everybody blames everything on covid." That was the angry me—which definitely was a shift because I didn't used to be like that.

A couple of days later, I got a call from the health department. And I thought, *Oh no, she's going to tell me I'm positive.* And she did. I had to sit down. I was like, "Are you sure?" She checked with their epidemiologists and called me back the next day. She said they were pretty sure it was a new strain. Pretty sure, but not 100 percent.

We quarantined and I got through it fine, except I was really tired. I also had some issues with my heart and felt like I was going to pass out a couple times.

In the midst of all this, my mom, who has Parkinson's disease, was diagnosed with Lewy body dementia. I've been seeing a therapist since the beginning of 2020, but all of this together—covid, my hand, my mom—it was too much. So I went to the doctor last week and got put on an antidepressant. I had to do it.

This past Friday, I started to have a fever and the chills. Then on Saturday, it started to hurt to breathe in. Yesterday morning, I called my doctor. They did a chest X-ray and found that I have a thickened airway from covid.

Last night, I was up all night. I was hardly able to sleep, because it's scary. They think they can fix it, but they don't know. And this is the thing, like everything that we're all going through right now, it's all unknown. It's all new territory, even for doctors. When you ask a doctor, they don't know necessarily if they can give you the solution. They're going through this with you.

I've learned through experiencing these hardships that it is okay not to be okay. You have to be able to say that, and you have to be able to move through all the hard stuff to heal. I look at my life a year ago, and I am a different person. I am more evolved, I think, spiritually and emotionally, because I'm able to get through hard stuff without blocking it out, without trying to cover it up and make it look pretty. And don't get me wrong, I love to make things look beautiful and I want to get back there, I do. I'm just not there yet.

Right now, I make things more beautiful by being with my daughter. The other day, I wasn't feeling well, but my daughter and I went outside because it's finally warming up. We made a little fairy garden in our backyard. It's simple things like that right now.

Wisconsin
May 2021

He looked at me and said, "What's long-haul COVID*?"*

Nick

Husband of COVID Long-Hauler

Heidi was a paragon of health. She ate organic food and walked ninety minutes a day. On January 1, 2020, she celebrated her two-year anniversary of being sober. She was in great shape.

I had the worst cough of my life that started in December and lasted for weeks. I had to ask my doctor finally for a steroid inhaler, which I had never used before in my life. Then, after deciding at the age of fifty that I should start skateboarding, I broke my collarbone skateboarding. Heidi was not happy about that and told me in no uncertain terms that it was the stupidest thing I've ever done. She was right about that because I'd fractured my thumb skateboarding ten days earlier.

I went back to work in early January when the cough went away. We had our offices in a communal, shared workspace, and when they sent us home March 12, they started sending us emails almost every day after that that somebody on the floor tested positive for COVID-19. I probably caught COVID either at work and brought it home or I was an asymptomatic carrier and brought it home. By April, Heidi was feeling weird. She had some weird digestive stuff and she got COVID toes. She thought we should go get tested, and we did the drive-through cheek swab test, the self-administered one where you have to shake up the vial yourself. We both tested negative, but they had a crazy-high fail rate.

She was starting to really show terrible signs. She had these pains in her feet that I thought were maybe plantar fasciitis because she was an avid walker. I said, "Honey, maybe you need new sneakers. You're almost fifty now and our feet change. Let's go to a podiatrist." The podiatrist said, "I treat plantar fasciitis all the time and I don't think it's that." He sent her to a neurologist, and it took a while to get the appointment. By July, when she got in to see the neurologist, her feet were excruciating. The neurologist diagnosed her with small fiber neuropathy, which is usually something that strikes diabetics. She was not diabetic, hadn't been close to diabetic. But at this point, she could barely walk. She had to ice her feet all the time and put her feet on soft cushy blankets.

Then all these other symptoms started, like digestive issues that were just horrible and affected her most of the day for weeks. And then this terrible exhaustion started. Just walking up steps, she literally would ask me to carry glasses of water upstairs because it would tire her out so much. And then she got the general sort of aches and pains, like muscular aches and pains that people with long COVID get.

By September, she was pretty much convinced she had long COVID, and I was too. I had no doubt. She blogged about it, joined a lot of long-haul groups. Heidi was a very research-oriented person who shared what she learned so it could help other people. When our son had infantile scoliosis, Heidi spent years online counseling other parents about how they should find the right treatment. When she joined an anonymous organization for her alcoholism, she spent years helping other people as well. She got really involved in these long-haul support groups, and she spent hours and weeks doing that.

By December, she was building up her ability to walk. She could walk for up to twenty minutes at a time. Twenty minutes was significant because it allowed her to get outside and see nature again. On the days she couldn't walk, we would drive down the Pacific Coast Highway and set up these little beach chairs on the side of the highway and just sit in the sun. We would just watch the waves coming in and just talk about life. One day, this beautiful white egret walked right in front of us, and the ocean was just glistening behind it. Egrets usually don't get that close to people there; they stay far away. It just walked right in front of us. I remember that day well. A peaceful, beautiful day.

By March, she wasn't better yet, but she was improving, and she'd heard that the vaccine could really improve people with long-haul COVID. I had a friend who was connected guide us on how to get the vaccine as early as we could. Within a few weeks after the first vaccine, she was not feeling good. It was noticeable. She started getting these tremors and they were scary. Her arms and torso started to shake, Parkinsonian tremors almost. They were coming more frequently, and we videotaped them because we wanted to be able to show neurologists. I would have my camera ready almost all the time.

Then internal vibrations in her chest cavity would start at night. Heidi said it was like being plugged into an electrical socket or having somebody put a vibration device inside of your chest cavity and turning it on. It prevented her from sleeping; she couldn't sleep more than an hour at a time for three weeks in a row. Even taking a prescription sleep medication didn't work.

She was starting to feel like there was no way out, that she was only going to get worse. She would say, "I don't know how I'm going to get better. There are no doctors to go to." The Cedars-Sinai long-haul COVID clinic that opened in January of 2021 wouldn't even see her because she hadn't had a positive test. I emailed her general practitioner and begged him. And he said, "They won't see her. There's nothing I can do." Heidi being the researcher that she was, she found this clinic up in Northern California that had developed a test for cytokine panels that was more detailed and sensitive and specific. They felt that those panels would accurately show people who had been exposed to COVID. When she got the results, we sent them to her doctor and the doctor sent an email saying that the levels were high enough that he was going to write a letter of referral to the Cedars clinic. Ironically, that arrived the day before she took her life.

I think she knew that she was only going to get worse and that medical science wasn't moving quickly enough. She didn't want to get worse. She'd say, "I don't want to lose the ability to walk. I don't want somebody to have to bathe me." I tried to be positive with her and say that medical science was moving faster than ever before. We got vaccines in a year and before that it would've taken four years.

It had gotten to the point that her bad days far outnumbered her good days. She could hardly eat anything, had trouble digesting, and was losing weight so fast. She was literally drinking olive oil and flaxseed oil as calorie replacement because she was losing so much weight. And she couldn't really get out of bed anymore because her heart rate would go from 80 to 130 within fifteen seconds of getting out of bed.

She was despondent. We'd been to the neurologist the day before it happened. The neurologist had tried to be positive and optimistic, but I could see they were concerned. One of them, a young male intern, tried to tell Heidi that it was just that she was depressed, that it was in her head. She turned to me when he walked out and said, "Did you see that? He was gaslighting me." He was. It was horrific. But then the older female doctor came in and really listened to her, acknowledged the physical pain, and said, "It's going to take time. We're not going to be able to solve this right away, but I do believe we're going to find the answers." She prescribed her some Lyrica to deal with her pain and help her sleep.

The day it happened, that morning she asked me to stop on the way back home from our son's playdate to get her some soup. She said, "I'm kind of hungry actually." I said, "That's good!" You know, it's good. She said, "Some really good soup. Like a good matzo ball soup from the deli. Would you mind?" I said, "I'm happy to." I got this big container of matzo ball soup and brought it home. I was so happy to see her eating.

That afternoon, I went to get the prescription for her. I brought it back and she was really despondent and sad. I tried to cheer her up. We bounced back and forth between how positive she should be. And she just said that I didn't understand.

I went to pick up our son. I don't know if I had a premonition, but when I picked him up, I told him to sit in the front seat, which I only do when I need to talk to him. I said, "Your mom has not been doing well." He said, "Yeah, I know." I said, "I want to believe that everything is going to be okay with her. I really do. I just can't guarantee it. I can't guarantee that she is going to be okay." He said, "Yeah, I understand." I said, "I just want you to know that no matter what happens here, we make a great team. We always have. No matter what happens, we're going to be okay." We got home. We walked up the steps to the second floor together; our bedroom is on the left. It wasn't unusual for the door to be closed. I said "Hon, we're back."

I'm going to stop there.

We followed the ambulance to the hospital, and we waited for the ER doctor to come out and talk to me. He said, "I'm so sorry. How long was your wife depressed?" I said, "She wasn't depressed. She did this because she was in excruciating physical pain for months from long-haul COVID." He looked at me and said, "What's long-haul COVID?" I said, "Are you kidding?" He goes, "No, I don't know what it is." I said, "Just Google it."

California
July 2021

*There was a stretch there, honestly, when I wasn't
sure if I was going to be able to make it all the
way back to where I was.*

Ron

Trombonist

On January 1, 2020, I was playing with the
Birdland Big Band in New York City as part of my regular one-week
residency between Christmas and New Year's Day. January and February were busy doing some performances with the Dizzy Gillespie
All-Star Big Band, playing on Broadway and a couple of other shows,
and trying to get in on *Aladdin*. I also was spending a lot of time in the
recording studio, getting ready to release my album by early summer.
I finally got the opportunity to play with the Broadway touring show of
Aladdin for a two-week run in Austin starting in March. Before I left
New York, there had been some COVID cases over at Yeshiva University,
which was only about three blocks away from me. I was concerned
about that, so I said to my gal, "I'm going to be going down to Texas,
and depending on how things look up here in New York, I'll probably
stay down there for a while. If things get too crazy, you should come
down as well and we'll be away from the epicenter."

Everything was going well, but around mid to late March, I noticed
my mom was getting a bit more lethargic and having trouble getting out
of bed. My mom started feeling better, and then I started feeling worse.
At first, I thought it was just allergies. One day in early April, my older
brother came into the bedroom and found me passed out, unresponsive.
I don't remember much, but the doctors said that I was going up and
down for the first three to four days. I was looking like I was getting better, then everything just crashed. They put me into a medically induced
coma, which I was under for thirty-seven days. I had the ventilator vent,
too. I was completely out of it. It's a blank spot in my memory.

By the time they brought me out of the coma, I had lost a fifth of my body weight. I went in weighing around 208, and I came out weighing maybe 165 pounds. I looked like a skeleton. I couldn't walk, couldn't talk, could hardly move my hands. I had the tracheostomy tube in my neck and a ventilator in my mouth. About two months before, I had lost three or four of my friends in New York who were very fine musicians, and all of a sudden, they were gone. It was scary.

I spent about another week in the ICU and then was transferred to a rehabilitation and specialty hospital. That's when I met some of the most courageous doctors, nurses, and therapists, some of the most incredible people I've ever known in my life. It took about another five weeks. I told the doctors and nurses that my goal was to put together a little jazz combo and come back and play for them sometime around Thanksgiving. They loved that idea. Part of my concern, of course, was whether I would be able to make music and whether I would be able to sing again. I was determined to be able to make my music again as a low brass musician, as well as a jazz vocalist and a composer. I made up my mind that I was not going to give up. My determination levels went through the roof. I knew that I was going to eventually get back to New York, I was going to continue my career, and I was going to focus on releasing my album.

I spent one more week in a more aggressive rehabilitation center. There, I started doing what we call "buzzing exercises." What I do as a brass player is I learn how to shape my lips into what we call our "mouth shape," and we try to get vibration through the lips. I was able to do buzzing exercises without the mouthpiece and that felt good. I was making progress.

I was released after about six days and then started outpatient therapy, both physical and occupational. I was in that for about another six weeks. When I finally finished up it was June 19. I had gone into the hospital on April 4 and finished up outpatient therapy around June 19.

I obviously wasn't working during that time, so I was on unemployment. My veteran benefits covered some of my healthcare costs, but as a musician, I didn't have regular health insurance to cover the gap. My partner and one of my former voice students put together a fundraiser for me, which raised a sizable chunk of money. People all over the world were contributing. It was amazing. And people were praying for me, chanting and lighting candles while hoping for the best and sending love and support. With the money raised, my partner and I were able to buy a car, so I was able to go back and forth to my appointments.

I picked up my trombone again the weekend of June 20. The first thing I played was "Lift Every Voice and Sing." I still have the video, and it sounded pretty good, which surprised me.

I played my first live gig again in early November, where I was a guest artist at St. James' Episcopal Church in Austin, Texas, for their Jazz at St. James' festival. I sang songs that are coming out on the album, and I played tenor trombone, bass trombone, and tuba. The craziest thing about it is that I figured I would be able to get through okay, but I was exhausted when I finished that. When I finished, my partner came up to me and said, "Are you okay? It sounded great, I couldn't believe how much you did." And I was like, "I have to sit down." I was just exhausted.

After the festival, I got calls from some friends of mine who had recording projects they wanted me to do online, including one with Charlie Rosen and the 8-Bit Big Band. Being able to do stuff like that again just really gave me this overwhelming sense that I'm back. I'm back and I'm not going to stop. And I've got more to do. By December 2020, I was back playing and working on my album.

I also was working on getting better physically and getting my head back on. There was a stretch in time for a little bit where I felt it was best for me to talk with a therapist so I could get a grasp on what I went through. When you lose time like that and then you come back from it, you're not the same as you were before. I didn't realize how much that would really affect my mental state. The therapy helped me realize and appreciate what I had been through and where I'm at now. I am literally filled with gratitude each day for being able to live, work, breathe, do, and make even more music than I have before.

I finally got back to New York this summer. When I left in March 2020, I had no idea what was ahead of me and that I wouldn't see my city again for over a year. Flying into New York for that first time in so long was . . . well, I cried a little. Looking down, seeing the World Trade Center, seeing the Financial District, seeing all the different skyscrapers, I cried a little. I cried in part because I was so excited to see the city that I love so much. But the other thing was that I came to this realization of what I had gone through to get back. It really overwhelmed me for a minute. It felt like I was back home. I can't tell you how many times I teared up even just walking from a friend's place in Harlem to the subway. Just to be back in Harlem again, to witness the sights, the sounds, the smells, the people, and the culture.

My first gig in New York was in August, playing on Central Park's Great Hill with the Dizzy Gillespie All-Star Big Band. I got to play the music I love with the people I love, and I was so filled with gratitude. I was just filled with this incredible sense of thankfulness and appreciation of everybody who was around me and the legacy of the music, as well as just being able to pull my horn out of the case and play some notes and sound like I hadn't missed a beat. And that was powerful. That was really, really powerful. And now here we are in October, and my album is out. It turned into one of the best projects I've ever done. I had always dreamed of being able to do a recording working with some top-notch New York cats. The album is doing well: people are listening to it and it's climbing up the charts.

I am just so happy to have these opportunities again. There was a stretch there, honestly, when I wasn't sure if I was going to be able to make it all the way back to where I was. I didn't allow much room for doubt, but if you don't at least allow some of that thought process, then you're missing out on some things. The reality of my condition and what I went through still hits me to this day. But we keep going, we soldier on. I have been soldiering on since then.

The thing that really bugs me more than anything else is how many people there still are in this country who have bought in to the misinformation and the politics of all this, as compared to just really trusting in the science. And now we just surpassed 700,000 deaths. I don't get it, I just don't get it. We shouldn't have had to get this far, especially when we have the means in this country to work with the scientific community and the medical community and the pharmaceutical companies. We got the vaccines with, as they say, warp speed.

As far as being able to talk with people about it, it's not about me trying to tell people how to think or act. It's just that I've lived this thing. I've lived it, I've been through it. Honestly, it breaks my heart because this is such a horrible virus. It's been one hell of a ride, I have to say. I don't wish this on anyone.

New York
October 2021

Driving all over the United States was a lot better than staying in one place.

Michelle

Author

When 2020 started, I was telling people that I was so fortunate. My job was pretty darn great: I got to fly all over the country, go to different places, and meet with different people, all for a good cause.

Then, in mid-January, I had a physical manifestation of what we were all going to be going through with COVID. At ten o'clock one night, I couldn't hear out of one ear. I went to bed and had a dream that the world was spinning. I sat bolt upright in my bed, and of course, the world *was* spinning; I had something called labyrinthitis. They still don't know what virus causes this, but it attacked my eighth cranial nerve and took out my sense of balance and the hearing in my right ear.

A week later, I was using a walker and just trying to power through. My hearing at that point was at 32 percent. It might or might not come back. I reached out to a woman I knew who'd been deaf in one ear for most of her life. And in part, that's where this book came from— I wanted to hear her story and hear how she got through it, to hear that life was just fine on the other side. Inspired by her example, I soldiered on.

Then when COVID hit, the national events I was planning for our nonprofit could no longer happen and my job was eliminated. I started looking for work and submitted eighty-six customized cover letters between mid-March and mid-July. Nothing. By mid-July, I had nothing. To make matters worse, the lease on my house was up on July 31. I had no idea where, or when, I was going to find a job, so signing a lease on a new place was not an option.

On July 15, sitting in a Target parking lot, I finally said out loud to myself, "Girl, you have got to tell the movers where to take your stuff. Where are you going to live? What are you going to do?" The only solution that made sense was to move into the 2006 motor home I had road-schooled my kids in for ten months when they were little.

I needed a project, though, because the thought of sitting in the motor home and submitting cover letters each and every day scared the heck out of me. It hadn't worked for the past four months, so why would anything be different? Driving all over the United States was a lot better than staying in one place and hoping things were going to be okay.

So that's what I did.

Getting on the road is in my blood. I am now the third generation in my family to live in an RV full-time. When my grandfather lost his job in 1936, he bought a trailer, and he and my grandmother lived in it for three years. My mom and dad ended up buying a trailer, too, so they could take us kids on weekend getaways and vacations. I loved going to campgrounds and playing with a new batch of kids every time. When my parents retired and got bored of country club life, they traveled all over the U.S. in their motor home for seven years. My little kids and I were lucky enough to be able to join them on their travels, once for ten months and a second time for four months. That's how I ended up having the 2006 motor home.

The big question was what kind of project I was going to do while I was on the road. Sitting in that Target parking lot on July 15, the answer came to me pretty quickly. I was really curious about how people were doing, so I decided to interview people from all over the country and to share it out on social media and a website. My friend Charlotte built the *Who We Are Now* website for me, and then I headed west.

I have to admit that as I got ready for the trip, I was concerned that this country was not the country I had grown up in. There was so much anger everywhere—at least, that's the way it seemed based on the news. I didn't know if I was driving out into a place that I could call home. I didn't know how it was going to feel or how people were going to receive me. I didn't know if people would want to talk about politics or masks or if it would be more about the regular stuff, like families and jobs.

I was hopeful that I could find ways to connect with most people.

What I had going for me was all those years growing up around camp-grounds and the fact that I was part Yankee, part southerner; part fairly recent to the U.S., part here since 1700; raised by parents who grew up working class and achieved the American dream. On the political front, I had been all over the map, volunteering for Jimmy Carter in middle school, working for George H. W. Bush's reelection campaign in 1992, and volunteering for campaigns for Democrats after I moved to North Carolina in 2000.

When I started my trip, my first stop was a campground in the Appalachian Mountains. I have always found it so easy to strike up con-versations with people in campgrounds. Well, not this time. I crashed and burned. Most people were sticking near their campsites and not walking about or hanging out at the playground. With my Who We Are Now brochure in hand, I approached some people at their sites and asked them, "Hi, can I talk with you?" And they're like, "What's wrong with you?" *Oh no*, I thought, *this is going to be a lot harder than I imagined.* State after state, my luck didn't get much better. What I was trying was not working.

Who I am at my core is a person who really enjoys hearing others' stories, understanding where they're coming from. Once I figured that out, I threw away the brochures and got to be myself in a way that was joyful and unscripted. Then everything started to roll. Because you know what? A lot of us want to hear each other's stories.

Many people in the more rural parts of the country asked me, "How's everybody else? How are people doing out there?" They knew their wide-open spaces and lower community densities had given them the ability to continue on with life in a more normal way and that peo-ple in the cities had not been as fortunate. I will never forget talking with Calvin, a cattle rancher in Alpine, Texas, who had stopped on the side of the road to help me fill the air in my tires. When he said to me, "I have been wondering about those restaurant owners in New York City," you could tell he really meant it. It wasn't just chit-chat; he had been thinking about it for a while. So, with Calvin, just like with everyone else who asked, we settled in and I answered his questions, stitching together stories of people from all over the country.

This has been a crazy, confusing time for everyone. It's kind of crazy the way that things happen. I've discovered that, at first, you don't know whether something's good or bad. I thought it was bad that I didn't have a job in July 2020. But it ended up being a good thing.

I have this story—it's my all-time favorite—that I was told by a guy who was in his early sixties. He'd spent his life trying to find the cure for cancer. "There was this couple, very much in love," he told me. "And they went to visit these beautiful cliffs overlooking the ocean. They went to a rock garden nearby, and there were lots of buses and pulled-up tourists. The couple became curious, and they walked around hand in hand to look at the rocks. *It's pretty,* they think, *but why are so many people here? What is so special about this rock garden?*

"And someone there told them, 'No matter where you stand, you can't see all the rocks.' They walked around some more, and sure enough, no matter where they stood, they couldn't see all the rocks. By and by, they dropped hands and each kind of meandered off. At some point, they were each standing at opposite ends of the rock garden. When they looked at each other, they realized that, between the two of them, they could see everything, all the rocks in the garden."

I was driving down the road, I don't remember which state I was in, when I realized, "Oh my God, I'm doing my rock garden." I called my daughter and said, "Kristin, I'm doing my rock garden. I'm finally doing my rock garden." And she said, "Yeah, you are, Mom. Didn't you realize that? By talking to all these people, you are going to see it all."

I wish I could have seen it all. By driving around the country, I got glimpses into so many lives. Now I know a little bit about what it must be like to be a ballet dancer on a football field in the middle of Yuma, Arizona, dancing the *Nutcracker*, because it's the only place where you can dance outside. I don't know exactly what it is like, but I have a little window into it.

I now know what I want to do for the rest of my life. I'll never see as many views of the rock garden as I want to.

North Carolina
July 2021

Acknowledgments

First and foremost, I want to thank the people along the way who took the time to sit down and tell me about their lives during the pandemic. We truly "are all in this together."

My parents and kids cheered me along my route and checked in to see how I was doing. My dog, Buddy, let me cuddle with him and talk to him any time of the day or night. Many thanks are owed to my mom and my cousin, Brian Shane, who read every single story and provided detailed feedback. My editors, Lucas Church at UNC Press and Alexa Dilworth at the Duke Center for Documentary Studies, helped me see things through a different lens, which made the book stronger. As a final note, I should thank "The Turtle," my 2006 Fleetwood Jamboree, which carried my children and me across the country during our homeschooling years and has now provided me with an open, expansive window to my future.